A LETTER TO STRESSED COMMUNITIES

A LETTER *to* STRESSED COMMUNITIES

Inverted Values in Inverted Parallelisms

GRAEME FINLAY

WIPF & STOCK · Eugene, Oregon

A LETTER TO STRESSED COMMUNITIES
Inverted Values in Inverted Parallelisms

Copyright © 2025 Graeme Finlay. All rights reserved. Except for brief quotations in critical publications or reviews, no part of this book may be reproduced in any manner without prior written permission from the publisher. Write: Permissions, Wipf and Stock Publishers, 199 W. 8th Ave., Suite 3, Eugene, OR 97401.

Wipf & Stock
An Imprint of Wipf and Stock Publishers
199 W. 8th Ave., Suite 3
Eugene, OR 97401

www.wipfandstock.com

PAPERBACK ISBN: 979-8-3852-6249-6
HARDCOVER ISBN: 979-8-3852-6250-2
EBOOK ISBN: 979-8-3852-6251-9

VERSION NUMBER 11/03/25

Copyright © 2025 Graeme Finlay.

Scripture translations have been taken from Good News Translation® (Today's English Version, Second Edition) © 1992 American Bible Society. All rights reserved.

Scripture translations have been taken from The Jerusalem Bible, published and copyright 1966, 1967 and 1968 by Darton, Longman & Todd Ltd. and Doubleday and Co. Inc.

Scripture translations have been taken from The New Testament in Modern English by J. B. Phillips copyright © 1960, 1972 J. B. Phillips. Administered by The Archbishops' Council of the Church of England.

Scripture translations have been taken from Holy Bible, New International Version®, NIV® Copyright ©1973, 1978, 1984, 2011 by Biblica, Inc.® All rights reserved worldwide.

Scripture translations have been taken from Revised Standard Version of the Bible, copyright © 1946, 1952, and 1971 the Division of Christian Education of the National Council of the Churches of Christ in the United States of America. All rights reserved.

CONTENTS

List of Figures | vii
List of Tables | viii
Introduction | ix
Abbreviations | xii

1. Jacob's Letter: Author and Context | 1
2. Structure: Parallelisms, Chiasms | 12
3. Adversity to Maturity | 22
4. Listening and Doing | 26
5. Prejudice or Love | 30
6. Faith and Actions | 34
7. Controlling the Tongue | 39
8. More on True Wisdom | 46
9. Community Health: Patience, Integrity, Prayer | 59
10. Summing up | 64

Appendix 1: Jacob's Letter as One Extended Chiasm | 71
Appendix 2: Chiasms Within a Chiasm | 75
Bibliography | 79
Index | 81

LIST OF FIGURES

Figure 1. Psalm 7 Arranged as a Chiasm | 14

Figure 2. The Story of Noah as a Palistrophe | 16

Figure 3. Adversity Promotes Growth to Maturity | 23

Figure 4. Listening Must Result in Doing | 27

Figure 5. Prejudice Negates Love | 31

Figure 6. Faith and Actions | 35

Figure 7. Controlling the Tongue | 41

Figure 8. True Wisdom | 44

Figure 9. Your Quarrels | 48

Figure 10. Your Criticisms | 51

Figure 11. Your Boasting | 54

Figure 12. Your Exploitation | 56

Figure 13. Patience, Integrity, Prayer: Health in the Community | 61

Figure 14. Jacob's Letter Is Structured as a Single Extensive Chiasm | 72

Figure 15. Patience Under Pressure | 76

Figure 16. Praying When Troubled | 76

LIST OF TABLES

Table 1. Jacob's Letter: Allusions to, or Echoes of, Jesus' Teaching | 4

Table 2. Jacob's Letter: Allusions to, or Echoes of, the Hebrew Scriptures | 6

Table 3. Chiasm-Defined Subdivision of Jacob's Letter | 19

Table 4. Understanding Verse 4:5 (D) | 50

Table 5. Foci of Jacob's Chiasms: A Distillation of the Way of Jesus | 66

Table 6. Parallel Features in the Chiastic Structure of Jacob's Letter | 73

INTRODUCTION

IN 2021, THE CITY in which I live was shut down because of the COVID-19 pandemic. Public health physicians were terrified that hospitals might become overwhelmed with people suffering from this novel, highly contagious, and potentially lethal disease. We could leave our homes only to purchase essential groceries and to walk locally in household groups for fresh air and exercise. For more distant social engagements, we were limited to online interactions through platforms such as Zoom.

That year, I was leading a Bible study group that was part of a vibrant multicultural inner city church, appropriately named the Global congregation. Whilst under lockdown, the decision was made to study the brief biblical letter ascribed to James. It seemed that this text was an appropriate resource for the situation because it is famously down-to-earth and packed with practical applications for people's life journeys, particularly when they are faced with difficulties. It provided insights on how to get on with other people when living under pressure—and for many, being cooped up with a small group of flatmates or family members made for a challenging environment.

Close attention to the letter of James was very enriching. For me at least, its very concrete concern with relationships in the body of Christ was an invigorating alternative to the social deprivation experienced during the lockdown period. The subject matter of this letter was a sweet breath of reality during an unprecedented crisis that many were finding to be surreal. I am very grateful to

A Letter to Stressed Communities

the members and pastors of the Global congregation for creating the opportunity for me to engage interactively in this challenging and relevant study. Life can dish up a diverse array of crises, unannounced and often hard to bear, and the letter of James can provide strength and direction in all those situations.

In addition, with the increased amount of time available, as I pored over the text of James's letter, I started to notice that many of the subsections appeared to fall into a striking pattern. A series of statements was given (call them A-B-C) that appeared to progress to a climax (D), then followed by a related series of statements, but in *reverse order* to the initial series (C'-B'-A'). This arrangement demarcated topical units, the paired elements highlighted themes, and the central focus identified especially significant teaching points. Such structures are known widely in ancient literature and are called *chiasmus* or *chiasms*.

Continued reflection led to the conclusion that essentially the entire text of the letter is composed of subsections arranged in this mirror-image pattern. Indeed, the letter in its entirety also has chiastic form. *Form* underlies *function*, and it seems that ancient readers would have been sensitive to textual *forms* (to which our literary education has not prepared us). These chiastic forms would have helped them to discern aspects of the *function* or *meaning* of the text.

The letter is a handbook of ethics for those who would follow the Way of Jesus. But our moral fiber is fragile. We are people of straw (to misquote Luther's assessment of the letter of James) for whom constant reminders are needed as to how we should live. We easily become preoccupied with the "wisdom" of the present age and overlook the essential insights of the past. Biblical precepts are shelved. If only we went so far as to put them into practice—with energy and urgency—then our lives, our communities, and indeed our world would have markedly different character. That is why this little letter, often overlooked at the back of the New Testament, is of such revolutionary importance.

It is essential that readers use this book with the Bible open before them. And the comments cannot be thought of as final or

Introduction

definitive. They are intended to be conversation-starters, to help each reader approach the letter with fresh eyes to see and an enhanced desire to put into practice the radical vision of Christlike behavior that it describes.

ABBREVIATIONS

BIBLE TRANSLATIONS

GNT   Good News Translation
JB   Jerusalem Bible
JBP   J. B. Phillips Translation
NIV   New International Version
RSV   Revised Standard Version

REFERENCE WORKS

IBC   *The International Bible Commentary.* 2nd ed. Edited by F. F. Bruce, et al. Basingstoke, UK: Marshall, Morgan & Scott, 1986.
IBD   *The Illustrated Bible Dictionary.* Edited by J. D. Douglas, et al. Leicester, UK: Inter-Varsity, 1980.
NBC   *The New Bible Commentary.* 4th ed. Edited by Donald A. Carson, et al. Nottingham, UK: Inter-Varsity, 1994.
WBC   *The Wycliffe Bible Commentary.* Edited by Charles F. Pfeiffer and Everett R. Harrison. London: Oliphants, 1963.

1

JACOB'S LETTER

Author and Context

THE LETTER OF JAMES is the first of seven short "general letters" in the New Testament. The letter writer has traditionally been identified as the brother of Jesus and an early leader of the church in Jerusalem. However, one issue invites consideration at the onset of our reflection on the letter. The name of the letter's author is a mistranslation that requires immediate remediation. The letter was sent from *Iakobos*, the Greek form of a Hebrew name that in English is *Jacob*.[1] The name *James* was substituted incorrectly for *Jacob* in an early English translation (that of John Wyclif, fourteenth century) and has stuck ever since. I have opted to follow scholarly recommendation and revert to the name of the sender as given in the original Greek, and as recognized in translations into languages other than English.

Mark Wilson emphasizes that it is important to revert to the author's true name for several reasons. First, it removes inconsistency from scholarly discourse. Why should *Iakob or Iakobos* be rendered *Jacob* when referring to the Old Testament patriarch but *James* when referring to people who lived in New Testament times?[2] Second, if the author was truly a son of Joseph who mar-

---

1. Wilson, "James or Jacob."
2. *Iakob* or *Iakobos* is translated *Jacob* in Matt 1:2, 15–16, 8:11; Luke 1:33,

ried Mary, his grandfather was named Jacob,[3] as was the famous ancestor of his race.[4] The author was named after his grandfather. There is pride in the family lineage—and presumably in the family's Jewish heritage. Third, Jacob was one of the most popular Jewish names of the period, and by neglecting to acknowledge this correct name, the author is removed from his cultural context. And fourth, this letter of Jacob is the most "Jewish" book of the New Testament, steeped in allusions to the Torah and the wisdom books of the Hebrew Scriptures (the Old Testament of the Christian Bible), and it had the familiar genre of a diaspora letter,[5] that is, a letter intended for any of the vast numbers of Jews who lived beyond the boundaries of their homeland. We should pay attention to its Jewish roots.

Jacob's letter provides no clear pointers as to when it was written. There is a lack of scholarly consensus as to the time of publication. Opinions have varied wildly. The letter does not contain clear reference to distinctively Christian doctrines, and this feature has suggested to some people that it is a "pre-Christian Jewish writing" that was adapted for Jewish-Christian use by the two-fold insertion of "the Lord Jesus Christ." This scenario would favor an early date in the first few decades of the history of the Way of Jesus. Other scholars have opined that the letter may address "the needs of more settled Christian communities," and if so, it would be dated more appropriately to a time following AD 70,[6] by which time the high priesthood (the hostility of which may be inferred from the text) had ceased to exist.

John Drane has considered arguments on both sides of the conundrum.[7] Consistent with an early date, he has noted that, first, the letter is addressed to "the twelve tribes," implying an early

---

3:34; John 4:12; Acts 7:8, 32; Rom 9:13; Heb 11:9, 20, but *James* in Matt 10:2–3, 13:55; Mark 3:17–18, 6:3; Luke 6:14–15; Acts 1:13, 15:13, 21:18; Jude 1.

3. Matt 1:16.
4. Matt 1:2.
5. Wilson, "James or Jacob."
6. *IBD* 732.
7. Drane, *Life*, 90–91.

period when followers of the Way of Jesus saw themselves simply as heirs of Israel's calling and faith. Second, there were no indications of a break between Jews and the (nascent) Christian community. Jacob rails against "the rich," who were probably fellow Jews. He condemned them for their ethics but not for their adherence to Jewish law or customs. In addition, it appears that his addressees gathered in the synagogue (2:2). Third, imagery reflects a Palestinian environment (such as reference to the "autumn and spring rains" [5:7]; anointing with oil [5:14]).[8] Fourth, concerns of the church from later times (such as those when Paul corresponded) were not raised. The letter does not refer to controversies between Jews and gentiles, concerns over heresies infiltrating the community, church order and doctrine, or introduced pagan morals.

On the other hand, Jacob's letter has a famous section on faith and actions (2:14–26) that some have understood to be a corrective to Paul's emphasis on faith. This implies that Jacob wrote after Paul. However, there is no evidence that Jacob and Paul knew each other's writings. In any case, the notion that Jacob and Paul opposed each other with respect to the relative importance of "faith" and "actions" cannot be sustained by closer analysis of their arguments.[9]

Drane proposed that Jacob's letter circulated very early in the life of the church. He suggested that it reflects the needs of the first disciples of Jesus in rural Galilee. But Drane remained noncommittal about the identity of "Jacob."[10]

WHO WAS JACOB?

Certain features of the letter are eminently compatible with the hypothesis that the author was Jacob, the brother of Jesus and leader of the Jerusalem church. The letter shares abundantly with material given in Matthew's Gospel and particularly with Jesus'

---

8. See also Mark 6:13.
9. Drane, *Life*, 92–93; Evans, *Jesus to the Church*, 88–93.
10. Drane, *Life*, 89–90, 92.

teaching as given in the Sermon on the Mount (table 1).[11] Jacob's letter includes more of the words of Jesus than all the other letters in the New Testament combined.[12] Indeed, White is sympathetic to the view that Jacob's letter is essentially a series of meditations on the words of Jesus.[13] As Davids states, "There is no better example in the NT of a church leader taking the Lord's teaching and applying it to church problems."[14]

The way Jesus' teachings are presented implies that Jacob received and delivered the same oral traditions as did the writer of Matthew's Gospel.[15] The close congruence in the way by which Jacob and Matthew reported the teaching of Jesus is strong evidence that the oral traditions they received authentically reflected the words spoken by Jesus, and that these writers were careful and accurate in the way they wrote them down and applied them for later readers.[16]

Table 1. Jacob's Letter: Allusions to, or Echoes of, Jesus' Teaching[17]		
Teaching	Jacob	Gospels
Believers find joy in trials	1:2	Matt 5:10–12 // Luke 6:22–23
Endurance leads to maturity, perfection	1:4	Matt 5:48
God gives generously	1:5, 17	Matt 7:7–11 // Luke 11:9–13
Pray in faith, not with doubt	1:6	Mark 11:22–24 // Matt 21:21
Faithfulness in trials leads to God's gift of life	1:12	Matt 10:22; Mark 13:13 // Matt 24:13

11. Barclay, *Letters*, 26; *IBD* 733; Drane, *Life*, 88.
12. See Carson, "James," in *IBC* 1533.
13. White, *Biblical Ethics*, 207.
14. See Davids, "James," in *NBC* 1354.
15. Wright and Bird, *New Testament*, 735.
16. Jacob seems to draw on at least three of the strands of source material regarding Jesus that contributed to the synoptic Gospels: Mark, Matthew-Luke ("Q") and Matthew-only ("M").
17. Wright and Bird, *New Testament*, 742.

Table 1. Jacob's Letter: Allusions to, or Echoes of, Jesus' Teaching[17]		
Teaching	Jacob	Gospels
Human anger does not achieve God's purposes	1:20	Matt 5:22
Do not merely listen to but obey God's word	1:22–25	Matt 7:24–27 // Luke 6:46–49
The poor, rich in faith, inherit God's kingdom	2:5	Matt 5:3 // Luke 6:20
Law of the Kingdom: "Love your neighbor"	2:8	Mark 12:31 // Matt 22:39; Luke 10:25–28
Break one commandment to be a lawbreaker	2:10	Matt 5:19
Be merciful to receive mercy	2:13	Matt 5:7
A tree is known by its fruit	3:12	Matt 7:17–18 // Luke 6:43–44
Peacemakers are commended, blessed	3:18	Matt 5:9
The pure in heart are blessed	4:8	Matt 5:8
God exalts those who are humble	4:10	Matt 23:12; Luke 14:11; 18:14
Do not judge others	4:11–12	Matt 7:1–5; Luke 6:37
Rich people will lament	5:1	Luke 6:24
Do not hoard riches	5:2–3	Matt 6:19 // Luke 12:33
The dangers of hoarding riches	5:4–6	Matt 6:24–25 // Luke 16:13
The Lord's coming is imminent	5:8–9	Mark 13:24–27 // Matt 24:30–33 // Luke 21:25–27
The prophets were patient in suffering	5:10	Matt 5:12 // Luke 6:23
Do not take oaths	5:12	Matt 5:33–37
Restore someone who is straying	5:19–20	Matt 18:15; Luke 17:3

Some terms used in Jacob's letter are like those attributed to Jacob of Jerusalem in the Acts of the Apostles. In the introduction to Jacob's letter, people are greeted with the word *chairein*; the only other time this word was used in church correspondence in the New Testament was the circular letter authorized by Jacob of Jerusalem.[18] Jacob the letter writer addresses his hearers with the call "Listen, my brothers," as does Jacob of Jerusalem.[19] Jacob the letter writer and Jacob of Jerusalem speak of believers as being those who "are called by the name" of their Lord.[20] And Jacob in each setting quotes from the Greek translation of the Hebrew Scriptures (the Septuagint).[21]

Jacob's writing was also deeply Jewish. He drew extensively from the Hebrew Scriptures, especially from the law and wisdom literature. Craig Evans has provided a compendium of allusions to the Hebrew Scriptures in Jacob's letter (table 2). The list is said to be merely illustrative, not comprehensive.[22] It is natural to see Jacob as one of the believers of Jerusalem, who were all "zealous for the law" as late as Paul's visit to the city after his third evangelistic journey, which was probably in AD 57.[23]

Table 2. Jacob's Letter: Allusions to, or Echoes of, the Hebrew Scriptures[24]		
Teaching	Jacob	Hebrew Scriptures
Seek wisdom	1:5	Prov 2:3–6
The faithless are like a turbulent sea	1:6	Isa 57:20
Our transience is like grass that withers	1:10–11a	Ps 102:4; 103:15–16
The need to control the tongue	1:26	Ps 34:13; 39:1; 141:3
Do not favor those who are wealthy	2:1	Job 34:19
Love your neighbor as you love yourself	2:8	Lev 19:18
Do not show partiality	2:9	Deut 1:17

---

18. Jacob 1:1; see also Acts 15:23; Barclay, *Letters*, 27; *IBD* 733.

19. Jacob 2:5; see also Acts 15:13; *IBD* 733.

20. Jacob 2:7 and Acts 15:17; Barclay, *Letters*, 27; *IBD* 733.

21. Jacob 1:10–11, 4:6; and Acts 15:16–18; see Carson, "James," in *IBC* 1534. This feature is of limited evidential value as the use of the Septuagint was widespread.

22. Evans, *Ancient Texts*, 342.

23. Acts 21:20; see Carson, "James," in *IBC* 1533. The date is from Wright and Bird, *New Testament*, 363.

24. Evans, *Ancient Texts*, 399–401.

Table 2. Jacob's Letter: Allusions to, or Echoes of, the Hebrew Scriptures[24]

Teaching	Jacob	Hebrew Scriptures
The law condemns adultery and murder	2:11	Exod 20:13–14; Deut 5:17–18
Abraham prepared to offer Isaac	2:21	Gen 22:9, 12
Abraham believed God, accepted as righteous	2:23	Gen 15:6; 2 Chr 20:7
Rahab	2:25	Josh 2:1–21; 6:17
Tongues like poison	3:8	Ps 140:3
People made in the likeness of God	3:9	Gen 1:26–27
Righteousness yields peace forever	3:18	Isa 32:17
God is a jealous God	4:5	Exod 20:5
God gives grace to the humble	4:6	Prov 3:34
Come near to God, God will come near to you	4:8	Zech 1:3; Mal 3:7; Isa 1:16
Humble yourselves and God will lift you up	4:10	Job 5:11
Do not boast about tomorrow	4:13–14	Prov 27:1
Pay your workers their wages	5:4	Deut 24:14–15
The wicked are like sheep ready for slaughter	5:5	Jer 12:3; 25:34
The Lord sends autumn and spring rains	5:7	Deut 11:14; Jer 5:24; Joel 2:23
Those who endure are blessed	5:11a	Dan 12:12
The Lord is full of compassion	5:11b	Exod 34:6; Ps 103:8; Ps 111:4
Elijah prayed, no rain fell	5:17	1 Kgs 17:1
Elijah prayed, rain fell	5:18	1 Kgs 18:42–45

Jacob's letter also contains a wealth of ideas connected with Greco-Roman literature and with Hebrew writings that are not present in the Bible. The writer was clearly deeply Jewish and also had imbibed extensively from a Hellenistic cultural environment. The confluence of traditions emanating from Jewish history, from Jesus, and from the wider Greco-Roman world situates Jacob in the earliest Jewish-Christian era of the church—presumably up to, but not beyond, the conflagration of the Jewish war (AD 66–70).

ISSUES RAISED TO QUESTION JACOB AS BROTHER OF JESUS

First, some writers have questioned the identity of Jacob as brother of Jesus on the basis of a supposed lack of specifically Christian teaching (despite its many allusions to the ethical teaching of Jesus). The content of any letter is strongly influenced by its context. This letter is primarily a work of ethical instruction to communities under duress. The abuse took the form of "economic persecution and oppression." In response to such maltreatment, people "can either pull together and help each other or they can compromise with the world and split apart into bickering factions."[25] This letter urges the people to strengthen unity.

Hegesippus, a second-century church writer, described Jacob of Jerusalem (called *the Just*) as a man who was devout and who prayed earnestly and at length in the temple for the salvation of his people (so developing "calloused knees like a camel"). Jacob was widely respected by the populace. Hegesippus's account may be largely legendary, but it paints the picture of a man of deep piety.[26] This coheres with the idea that Jacob the letter writer was by nature a moralist rather than a theologian.[27] He was concerned about the way in which faith is lived, not how it is described abstractly. There is no reason why anyone should baulk at Jacob's ethical content. Even today, theologians separate themselves into systematists and ethicists.

In any case, Christian doctrine is indeed present through the letter. Jesus is described as "glorious" (2:1), presupposing his vindication in resurrection and ascension (and implying a recognition of his divinity). The writer goes to considerable effort to explain

---

25. See Davids, "James," in *NBC* 1354.
26. Barclay, *Letters*, 14–16.
27. See Carson, "James," in *IBC* 1533.

how authentic faith makes people righteous before God (2:14–26). Jacob recognized that he and his flock were living in "these last days" (5:3): the promised new covenant of the messianic age had been inaugurated.[28] The Lord's coming (*parousia*) is anticipated (5:7). It is suggested that the judge who is soon to appear (*parousia*, again) is Jesus himself (5:8–9). The life-giving work of the Spirit and the sovereignty of God in salvation are implied (1:18). Jacob alludes to the authority of elders (*presbuteroi*) and of ordered functioning churches (*ekklesia*) (5:14).[29] Christian presuppositions pervade the letter, even if the writer was not concerned to expound them explicitly.

Second, it has been proposed that the name and authority of "Jacob" were assumed pseudonymously by an author whose real identity has been hidden. Pseudonymity was very widespread in ancient times. Its purpose was to claim the authority or prestige of a past luminary for a freshly written work. But there are cogent arguments against this possibility. Jacob was a common name and its use without honorific predicates would have counted for nothing. An author seeking to cash in on apostolic authority would have specified "Jacob the brother of Jesus" or "Jacob who met the resurrected Lord" or "Jacob the apostle of Jerusalem." But there is no such claim, and the letter lacks features of pseudonymity (such as fictional embellishments).[30]

Indeed, the opposite mindset may underlie this letter. Jacob the Just of Jerusalem feels so unworthy to be representing his glorified Lord that in giving own his name, he underplays his credentials. He is but a servant (1:1) who desires to direct attention away from himself and towards the Lord who has called him.

Third, people have questioned that Jacob could be the brother of Jesus because the letter is written in polished Greek. Might we expect such literary sophistication of a rustic who originated in

---

28. Acts 2:17; 2 Tim 3:1; Heb 1:2; See Wessel, "James," in *WBC* 1438; König, *Eclipse*, 4.

29. See Carson, "James," in *IBC* 1533; White, *Biblical Ethics*, 208–9; Wright and Bird, *New Testament*, 732–33.

30. *IBD* 732–33; Wright and Bird, *New Testament*, 734–35.

provincial Galilee? There are several plausible scenarios that could accommodate Jacob's presumed sociocultural background with the quality of the Greek expression. Galilee was strongly Hellenized, and it might be expected that much of the populace would have been bilingual.[31] Jerusalem also was a cosmopolitan city, and from the earliest days, the church included a considerable number of Hellenistic (Greek-speaking) Jews.[32]

Jacob's letter was not an *occasional* letter, such as a person might write to a friend. It was an open letter, sent to a potentially broad, unrestricted general audience. As such, it was more like a *literary* letter, a formal tract. Indeed, parts have the character of structured sermons that Jacob may have delivered; he may have commissioned an editor competent in Greek to compile his outlines into the written form of an encyclical.[33] This suggested history of publication is eminently compatible with the structural analysis proposed below in this study.

Jacob's letter may have been written in Aramaic and subsequently translated into Greek. However, it does contain examples of both Semitisms and of Greco-Roman rhetoric such as the diatribe,[34] so it is safe to consider that the writer would have been thoroughly conversant with both Jewish and Greco-Roman culture. Jacob of Jerusalem readily conforms to this background.

Considering all the arguments, Wright and Bird have concluded that "the evidence marginally favours authenticity"—that is, that Jacob the brother of Jesus, early leader of the Jerusalem church, was the writer of this letter.[35] Craig Evans seems to be more confident. He states that Jacob and the first letter of Peter are "authentic and early letters, the former dating to the late 40s or early 50s" and that these letters "reflect an unmistakably Jewish,

---

31. Barclay, *Letters*, 39; *IBD* 732–33; Drane, *Life*, 89–92.
32. Acts 6:1–6.
33. See Davids, "James," in *NBC* 1355.
34. Wright and Bird, *New Testament*, 735.
35. In *New Testament*, 735; in this, they align themselves with eminent NT scholar Scot McKnight.

Palestinian flavour."[36] Jacob wrote at a very early stage of the Christian community "when there was little distinction between *synagoge* and *ekklesia*," when he could lead fellow Jews "towards the fulfillment of what God had promised Israel."[37] Evans's subsequent survey of the history of the nascent church is based squarely on the presumption of, and fits plausibly with, Jacob the Just of Jerusalem being the source of the letter.[38]

To conclude, Jacob's profile, his job description, seems to fit with the man who grew up with Jesus,[39] who at first rejected his messianic claims,[40] who met him in resurrection,[41] and who subsequently cared for the church in Jerusalem in the first three decades of its history.[42] But even if this attribution is incorrect, the letter will be pertinent to all people who follow Jesus and face hostility and hardship on this account, wherever and whenever they may be located. Jesus and Jacob both taught that the values cherished by human beings (the unbelieving "world") must be inverted to conform to the true values as they pertain to the kingdom of God. It is the poor and the persecuted who are blessed. It must be said that Western Christians face seduction, rather than persecution, by the world. On this account also, Jacob's letter is for them.

---

36. Evans, *Jesus to the Church*, 22–23.

37. Evans, *Jesus to the Church*, 37; for *synagoge*, see Jacob 2:2; for *ekklesia*, see Jacob 5:14.

38. Bauckham also shares Evans's confidence; see *Eyewitnesses*, 289 n90.

39. Mark 6:3 // Matt 13:55.

40. John 7:5.

41. 1 Cor 15:7.

42. Acts 12:17, 15:13, 21:18; Gal 2:9, 12.

2

STRUCTURE

Parallelisms, Chiasms

JACOB'S LETTER SEEMS TO be structured in ways that are typically Jewish. For this reason, it will be helpful to reflect briefly on some characteristics of Hebrew literary composition. Hebrew writing is noted for its *parallelisms*. Particularly in its poetry, the text is often written in doublets. Each of the elements comprising the doublet conveys a similar idea, although the second element may develop, or intensify, the sentiments expressed in the first. This pattern might be expressed A-A'-B-B'. For example, Ps 7 (to be analyzed chiastically below) commences,

> O LORD my God, I take refuge in you;
> save and deliver me from all who pursue me,
> or they will tear me like a lion
> and rip me to pieces with no one to rescue me. (vv. 1–2 NIV)

The first two lines feature the safety to be found in God. The second line (or *element*) expands the general idea of *refuge* to the concepts of *salvation* and *deliverance*. It introduces the tangible danger that is haunting the poet: enemies are pursuing him.[1] The following two lines express his fear that he might be physically

---

1. Traditionally, the poet is David; his slanderer, Cush (otherwise unknown), is likened to a lion. These animals survived in Palestine until the Crusades; Blaiklock, *Psalms*, 27.

injured (line 3)—indeed, that he might be torn to shreds. His situation is made more precarious by his anxiety that he is totally alone (line 4).

A more elaborate structure frequently encountered is known as *chiasmus* or a *chiasm*. This is a series of statements or ideas that is followed by an analogous series of statements, but in the reverse order. Such literary structures may also be called *inverted parallelisms*, or if they are particularly long, *palistrophes*. The basic form may be depicted for eight statements as,

$$A\text{-}B\text{-}C\text{-}D\text{-}D'\text{-}C'\text{-}B'\text{-}A'$$

in which A and A' are in some way parallel in vocabulary or relate to each other in meaning. The text develops towards, and then away from, the central theme (which may itself be stated once, or as shown above, in parallel; D, D').[2]

CHIASMS IN THE HEBREW SCRIPTURES

The chiastic pattern has been recognized for a long time in the wider ancient world[3] and in the Hebrew Scriptures. For example, in 1934, the book of Habakkuk was described as itself having some chiastic structure (ABA') and as containing a series of smaller chiasms.[4] This study also observed that chiasms are apparent in many of the Psalms. I have noted Ps 7 to be a clear example and have outlined the symmetrical mirror-image structure in figure 1.

---

2. Breck, "Biblical Chiasmus," 70; Bailey, *Jesus*, 13–18.
3. McCoy, "Chiasmus," 18–19, 22, 25.
4. Walker and Lund, "Literary Structure," 355–70.

A Letter to Stressed Communities

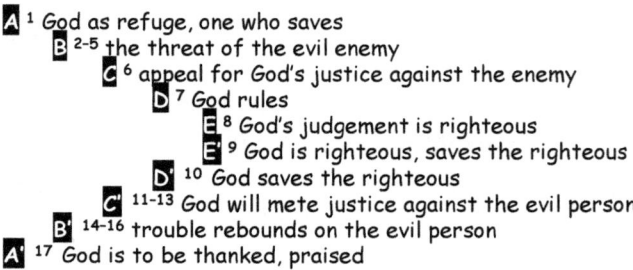

Figure 1. Psalm 7 Arranged as a Chiasm

The first and last elements (that is, A and A') are expressions of worship. In a threatening world, God is the one in whom we may find protection, safety, serenity (v. 1). It follows that gratitude and adoration are due to this God (v. 17). Whatever challenges are described in the psalm, whatever disturbs or terrifies the poet, the all-encompassing goodness of God provides the context for his hope-filled thinking and living.

The second and second to last elements (B, B') describe the problem. These elements are paralleled for their length and by their content: an enemy appears. In B (vv. 2–5), the author, considered to be David, is in anguish over the threats of an adversary, the animosity of whom he considers to be entirely unjustified. David's hands are clean, but it seems as if his enemy is intent on destroying him. In B' (vv. 14–16), David is confident that his adversary will self-destruct. He will fall into the trap he has made. His evil scheming will rebound on him. In this latter element, David is clearly more upbeat. What is the source of his confidence?

The next pair of elements (v. 6, C; vv. 11–13, C') bring God's justice to bear upon the situation and, in particular, on the machinations of the enemy. David is confident that God is filled with righteous anger against evil people, and David appeals to God's justice, knowing that such justice is inherent to God's very nature (vv. 6, 11). David's confidence is stressed in the next pair of elements: it is based on the assurance that God rules (v. 7, D) and God saves (v. 10, D').

STRUCTURE

The climax of the psalm is the close parallelism at the center. It expresses David's confidence that God will judge his people according to their righteousness (v. 8, E). God by nature is righteous and will protect those who are righteous (v. 9, E′).

Some might consider this psalm to be a "disconnected utterance," a "collection of succeeding emotions rather than of sequent thoughts," a "storm-tossed prayer."[5] However, when it is read as a chiasm, the writer's confidence in God when facing dark adversity is expressed in a very ordered way and is predicated upon God's justice/righteousness.

A particularly clear example of an extended palistrophe in the Hebrew Scriptures/Old Testament is furnished by the story of Noah, as originally noted by Gordon Wenham[6] and affirmed by him twenty-five years later.[7] In this story, there are fifteen elements on both sides of the central "hinge" or "pivot" (A to O, followed by O′ to A′). But why should the story be written in this highly symmetrical way? Wenham suggests, first, that the story "gives literary expression to the character of the flood event."[8] The rise of the flood to its peak is followed by its subsidence, in the same way as the ascent of the palistrophe to its climactic teaching point is followed by its descent back to normalcy. This structure highlights "the parallels between God's destructive work in sending the flood and his work of re-creation."[9]

Second, the central feature of the chiasm "draws attention to the real turning point in the saga, 'And God remembered Noah'. It was God's intervention that was decisive in saving Noah."[10] In the affirmation given in the climactic "hinge" statement, "God remembered Noah" (8:1a, P); God's authority, saving purposes, care, and righteousness are shown to be the focus of the story.

---

5. Blaiklock, *Psalms*, 27.
6. Wenham, "Coherence," 336–48.
7. Wenham, *Exploring the Old Testament*, 28.
8. Wenham, "Coherence," 339–40.
9. See Wenham, "Genesis," in *NBC* 66.
10. Wenham, "Coherence," 339–40.

A Letter to Stressed Communities

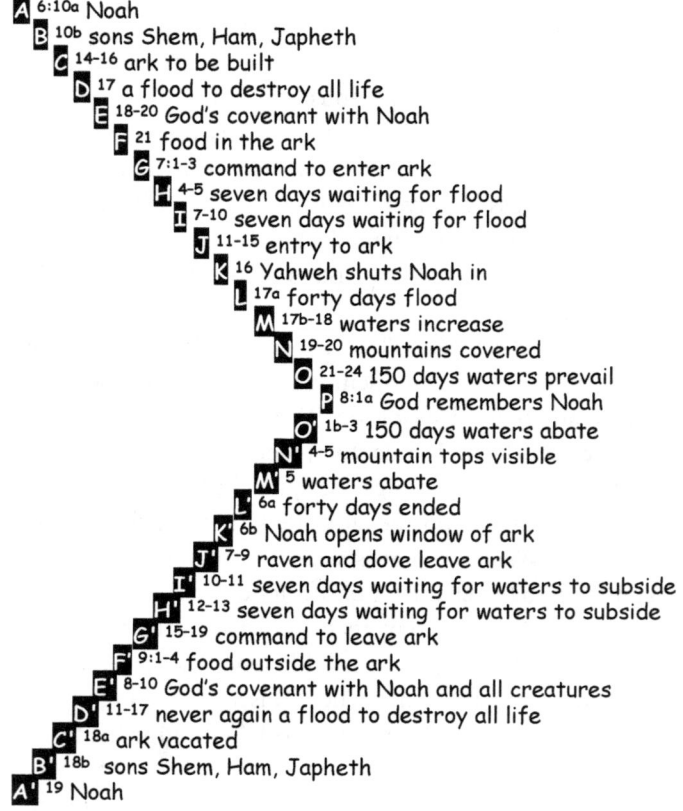

Figure 2. The Story of Noah as a Palistrophe

Another chiasm in Genesis describes a defining event in the story of Abraham: an encounter with God. As with the Noah story, the central climax focuses on the relationship between God and his servant. It highlights the giving of the sacred covenant.[11]

---

11. Gen 17:1–25. In brief, the A elements specify Abraham's age; B, God appearing to and leaving Abraham; C, God's first and fifth speeches; D, Abraham falling on his face; E, God's second and fourth speeches; F, the focus, God's third speech emphasizing the covenant; see McCoy, "Chiasmus," 28.

Structure

CHIASMS IN JACOB'S LETTER

Over the last few decades, it has been shown that most of the apostolic writers, "like many of their Hebrew and Jewish predecessors, relied heavily on *chiasmus* (or 'chiasm') to produce their literary work."[12] The present study proposes that Jacob's letter is composed largely (if not almost exclusively) of a series of chiasms. An awareness of such inverted parallelisms should assist readers in noting the natural divisions of the letter and in following the way the author's argument develops in each section. It follows that many ancient texts can appear to our sensibilities to be a jumble of themes and confusingly repetitive, but when read chiastically, they can be seen to possess elegant order.

Ancient texts (including those of the Greeks and Hebrews) lacked demarcation of sentences and paragraphs, punctuation, and upper and lowercase lettering.[13] It may be hypothesized that the symmetrical structure of chiasms served to inform readers as to how they might navigate their way through texts. This proposition is supported by scholarly opinion: chiasm was

> a seriously needed element of internal organization in ancient writings, which did not make use of paragraphs, punctuation, capitalization and other such synthetic devices to communicate the conclusion of one idea and the commencement of the next.[14]

Given that this convention was widely used, it suggests that ancient Jewish readers possessed a sensitivity to repeated words and concepts that was much more developed than is ours centuries later.[15]

Chiasms may also have served a mnemonic function. Once a reader had learned the sequence of elements in the ascending part

---

12. Breck, "Biblical Chiasmus," 70.

13. Stock, "Chiastic Awareness," 24–26.

14. Stock, "Chiastic Awareness," 23; quoted with approval by McCoy, "Chiasmus," 23.

15. "Rhetorical analysis [which includes the identification of chiasms] frees us from 1,650 years of dominance by chapter headings and 450 years of subtle control by verse numbers" (Bailey, *Jesus*, 17).

of the chiasm, it was relatively straightforward to remember the inverted sequence in the descending part. Further, comparing the content of a pair of elements (say A with A′) may indicate how they complement, and perhaps explicate, each other. Identification of A elements also helped to reveal the theme of what was to come; the final A′ element would indicate the conclusion of the chiastically defined unit.

The central "hinge" or "pivot" of each chiastic unit should also provide occasion for reflection on a significant issue in the author's mind.[16] If we fail to recognise the symmetry present in a chiastic text, "we tend to misread the 'conceptual centre' and consequently to distort the author's message."[17] Breck has stated that chiastic analysis "offers an indispensable key to determining the 'literal sense' of a text: the chief point or theme the author sought to convey."[18] He has concluded that "we should read Scripture according to the same principles by which it was composed."[19]

For want of a better word, Jacob's chiastic subdivisions could be designated as "homilies."[20] The validity of this approach seems to be supported by the observation that many of these putative sections (seven out of eleven) are introduced by an appeal to Jacob's "brothers." In other words, a block of text that is identified as being chiastic on the basis of its inverted parallel structure tends to commence with an appeal to "my brothers" (table 3). As noted above, the book of Acts also depicts Jacob as prefacing his utterances with "my brothers."[21] Perhaps Jacob characteristically used this form of

16. McCoy, "Chiasmus," 31.
17. Breck, "Biblical Chiasmus," 73.
18. Breck, "Chiasmus in the Gospel," 72, 75, 90.
19. Breck, "Biblical Chiasmus," 74.
20. A homily is a short sermon, generally with the aim of providing instruction in ethics: "a piece of spoken or written advice about how someone should behave, as for example, 'He launched into a homily on family relationships'" (*Cambridge Dictionary*). The term *homily* as used herein was adopted from Bailey, *Jesus*, 13.
21. Note "brothers," *adelphoi*, is not necessarily a male term but may also indicate friends, fellow believers, or near kinsfolk. See Vine, *Expository Dictionary*, 154–55.

address to introduce a sermon or homily.[22] The recurrence of this salutation supports the idea that Jacob's letter is a compendium of orated homilies he had delivered.

Table 3. Chiasm-Defined Subdivision of Jacob's Letter			
Homily	Verses	Topic	Introductory address
1	1:2–18	Adversity to maturity	"My brothers," 1:2
2	1:19–27	Listening and doing	". . . my dear brothers," 1:19
3	2:1–13	Prejudice or love	"My brothers," 2:1
4	2:14–26	Faith and actions	"My brothers," 2:14
5a	3:1–12	Controlling the tongue	"My brothers," 3:1
5b	3:13–18	True wisdom	
Diatribe 1	4:1–10	Your quarrels	
Diatribe 2	4:11–12	Your criticisms	"Do not criticize . . . my brothers," 4:11
Diatribe 3	4:13–17	Your pride	
Diatribe 4	5:1–6	Your exploitation	"Now you rich people," 5:1
6	5:7–18	Patience and prayer	"Be patient then, my brothers," 5:7

There are exceptions to the use of the "my brothers" convention in introducing a chiastically ordered homily. First, there are four putative chiasms that are not introduced by the "my brothers" formula. The first one (3:13–18) may in fact be a direct extension of 3:1–12, that is, it may function as an elaborated parallel of 3:1 (an A element) by stressing the character of a good teacher. The chiastic unit 3:13–18, then, may be an appendix (part of the corresponding A′ element) that describes the false wisdom that pertains to the world and the true wisdom from God that teachers should be diligent to manifest and model for their students.

Four generally short paragraphs follow in 4:1–10, 11–12, 13–17, and 5:1–6. Only the second is prefaced by an appeal to

---

22. Acts 15:13.

"my brothers," but these four may constitute a bracket of succinct diatribes in which the author engages polemically—indeed, heatedly—with an antagonist identified only as "you." The first three of these suggest Jacob has heard the news that at least some of the scattered communities of Jesus' followers were engaging in incessant bickering. Some have retained patterns of speech (that troublesome "tongue" again, see also 3:1–12) that come from the unbelieving world. Jacob roundly chastises those who engage in (respectively) quarrelling, criticism of each other, and arrogant claims of autonomy.

It may be a shock to discover that the first generation of Jesus' communities was so flawed. But of course, a very few years later, we discover the same difficulties in the churches for which Paul[23] and John of Patmos[24] were concerned. And as for us, *caveat lector*, let the reader beware! We in the twenty-first century should continually reflect on whether our influence in the church is loving and unifying and whether it contributes towards a community to which wary nonmembers are attracted. Jacob's letter is desperately relevant to us.

The fourth of the short chiasms is not an exception to the "my brothers" pattern because Jacob's condemnation is not directed to the believers at all. Jacob is here addressing the rich and powerful (*plousioi* [5:1]), the persecutors of his flock, and those who represent "the world" in all its corruption.[25] The objects of his censure are the Jewish plutocracy who comprised the ruling council (the Sanhedrin). It was they who oppressed the poor and weak and ruthlessly exploited their laborers. We would not expect him to address them as his "brothers," as he roundly denounced their avaricious and vicious ways.

Second, there are six cases of an address to "my brothers" without a following chiasm. The first and third seem to be impassioned appeals prefacing the summaries that conclude the

---

23. Gal 1:6; 1 Cor 1:11; 2 Cor 10:1–11.

24. Rev 2:1–7, 3:14–22.

25. "The term 'rich' (Gk. *plousios*) in James is used only for non-believers" (Davids, "James," in *NBC* 1358).

STRUCTURE

respective homilies (1:16; 3:10). The second, fourth, and fifth could be emphatic reinforcements of the central focus of the third and last homilies (2:5; 5:10, 12). And the last instance rounds off the letter (5:19) with a final brief word of encouragement (5:19–20).

Finally, it should be noted that analysis of the entire letter suggests that the whole is structured as one overall chiasm. Jacob's letter has a seven-part symmetry. This is a very significant number in Jewish thinking, indicating perfection or completion. Bailey has called this structure the "prophetic rhetorical template,"[26] and the scheme is presented in appendix 1. As we might expect, the central "hinge" paragraph is on faith and actions—it provides the definition of true faith—and the rest of this important little letter is commentary on how readers might nurture and apply that faith.

---

26. Bailey, *Jesus*, 138–39.

3

ADVERSITY TO MATURITY

THE FIRST SECTION OF Jacob's letter (1:2–18) addresses people who are challenged by difficulties in the form of persecution. It assures them that faithfulness to God results in the blessing of God. This homily is organized as a chiasm (fig. 3). The goal of surmounting trials is a humanity that is perfect (mature, fully developed) and complete, without deficiencies (vv. 2–4, A). The same sentiment is expressed at the end of the section (v. 18, A'). God gives a new quality of life to those who are obedient to him. They become his children, prototypical exemplars of the new creation. They may rejoice in these circumstances because there is a "future reward beyond the pain."[1]

Jesus taught values that invert those which humans assume to be self-evident. To the blind reasoning of the human mind, it is comfort, luxury, wealth, and self-gratification that are the means to a wholly fulfilled life. To Jesus, it was people who had lost their lives for Jesus' sake, and for that of the gospel, who would discover the full potential of humanness.[2] Jacob follows from Jesus by affirming that it is trials that lead to human perfection, the fulfillment of human nature (A).[3] The hard unrelenting struggle of resisting

---

1. Kaiser et al., *Hard Sayings*, 693.
2. Mark 8:35 // Matt 16:24–26 // Luke 9:23–25.
3. Probably reflecting Jesus' beatitude, "Blessed are you when people insult you, persecute you, and falsely say all kinds of evil against you. Rejoice and be

the demands of our appetites provides the conditions in which we may be elevated to first place among God's creatures (A'). That is, we receive the new birth[4] by means of "the word of truth," a term that probably refers to the gospel of Jesus (v. 18).[5] As a result, redeemed human beings are made "the apex of all creation."[6] Here, in one verse, Jacob summarizes Paul's lofty understanding of God's final purposes.[7] And Jacob is said to be a mere moralist?

> **A** 2-4 trials-endure-perfect-complete, lack nothing
>   **B** 5 lacks wisdom? God gives generously
>   **C** 6 doubt—passive wave of the sea
>   **D** 7-8 doubter receives nothing
>   **E** 9 poor, glad, God exalts
>   **E'** 10-11 rich, glad, God humbles
>   **D'** 12 faithful person receives life
>   **C'** 13-15 evil desire, temptation, sin—death
>   **B'** 16-17 deceived? God's good, perfect gifts
> **A'** 18 God gives being, first place among all creatures

Figure 3. Adversity Promotes Growth to Maturity

The second and penultimate elements are appeals to those followers of Jesus who are struggling, perhaps wavering, in the face of hardships. Jacob is concerned about those disciples who *lack wisdom* (v. 5, B) or are in danger of capitulating to *deception* due to the strain of the situation they are experiencing (vv. 16–17, B'). These parallel statements might indicate that to show a deficiency

---

glad because great is your reward in heaven" (Matt 5:11–12 // Luke 6:22–23); see also Paul (Rom 5:3–5) and Peter (1 Peter 1:6–7). Kaiser et al., *Hard Sayings*, 693.

4. John 1:13, 3:5–8; 1 Pet 1:23; 1 John 3:9, 5:18.
5. So defined in Col 1:5; 2 Tim 2:15.
6. See Davids, "James," in *NBC* 1358.
7. As the new humanity is the first, paradigmatic instance (*aparche*) of the new creation (Jacob 1:18), so is Christ the first instance (*aparche*) of resurrection (1 Cor 15:20–23), and the Spirit the first instance (*aparche*) of God's gifts flowing from the sacrifice of Christ (Rom 8:23).

in wisdom is to succumb to deception—to capitulate in the face of difficulty. Wisdom here is not philosophical speculation or abstract knowledge but the ability to live righteously.[8] When disciples of Jesus are in danger of buckling under the pressure, they should remember that God's *good gifts* are available to those who remain faithful. They are provided generously (v. 5, B) and are of the ultimate desirability because they are perfect (v. 17, B'), sourced from none other than the omnipotent Creator (vv. 5, 17). Peter Davids recognizes the connection between B and B', stating that "one example of such a good gift [v. 17] is the wisdom mentioned in v. 5, the parallel section."[9]

The alternative—to capitulate to the pressure—leads to disaster. To surrender to one's doubts is tantamount to opting for chaos, to becoming like a directionless, ephemeral wave of a stormy sea (v. 6, C). To be sculpted passively by one's environment—social, cultural, political—betokens the loss of all vitality. Jacob teaches that yielding to the syndrome of noncommitment/doubt-with-evil-desire is tantamount to choosing moral disaster and death (vv. 13–15, C').

The D elements reiterate the stark choice faced by Jesus' followers under pressure. Our choices determine whether we *receive* absolutely nothing on the one hand or the ultimate prize on the other—the gift of life itself. The doubter, the one who reneges on his or her commitment to Jesus, can *receive* nothing from God (vv. 7–8, D). The one who resists the temptation to give up and who remains faithful will *receive* the fullness of life as promised by God (v. 12, D').

The central elements have an air of paradox, enigma about them. Opposing states lead to the same end. Those who have cause to celebrate are both the poor lifted up and the rich brought down. The poor are brought into the infinite spiritual riches of Jesus the Messiah (v. 9, E). The domineering rich-laid-low have been granted the opportunity to escape from the shackles of materialistic privilege. They have been liberated from the burdens of their earthly riches. Or perhaps they represent members of the persecuting plutocracy who have discarded their riches and status and have adopted the

8. Barclay, *Letters*, 53.
9. See Davids, "James," in *NBC* 1358.

quest to follow Jesus. They have made the right choice to forsake wealth in order to become disciples (vv. 10–11, E′).[10]

Living in the materialistic West makes us oblivious to this inversion of priorities. We are allured by advertising and other media depictions of the "good life." Consumerist lifestyles are accepted unquestioningly as the norm. We become preoccupied, mesmerized, by the dream of affluence. Barclay states that the gospel "brings to every man what every man needs." The poor are elevated to a new sense of their own value. The rich experiencing abasement are rescued from their false sense of security and their perceived independence of others and of God.[11] Truly, the pursuit of riches—possessions, entertainments, and bank accounts—is a great impediment to spiritual responsiveness to the call of Jesus.

The poor and the downwardly mobile freed from their wealth may be refugees who have hastily left their homes and possessions in Judea and are now living in faithfulness to God. Persecution arises from human bitterness, pride, and hard-heartedness. God does not send oppression and brutality. In the same way, when we face sickness, accident, bereavement, injustice, or impoverishment, we must not assume these adversities come from God. Rather, God has devolved freedom upon the world. Bad things just happen. But our response to them makes all the difference. We can retreat into a mindset of self-pity, resentment, doubt, or anger towards God (the noncommitment/doubt-with-evil-desire syndrome). In doing so, our humanity shrinks, withers, perishes. Or we can exercise faith in God's continuing presence, love, and compassion. The God who raised Jesus from death brings new realities out of disasters. To respond in faith provides conditions in which God pours divine gifts into us, and so creates new beauty in us and through us.

---

10. An apparent paradox taught repeatedly by Jesus: people cannot serve God and money (Matt 6:19–21, 23–34), people should sell everything for a buried treasure or a beautiful pearl (Matt 13:44–46), rich people enter the kingdom of God only with difficulty (like the rich young ruler who could not bring himself to follow Jesus; Mark 10:17–31 // Matt 19:16–30 // Luke 18:18–30).

11. Barclay, *Letters*, 55.

4

LISTENING AND DOING

THE "MY DEAR BROTHERS" (or "dear family" or "dear friends") formula (v. 19) leads us to suspect we are entering a second chiasm-defined section or homily (1:19–27; fig. 4). The first and last elements address both positive and negative aspects of the readers' (or listeners') spiritual condition. If "behavior X" is expressed (positive) then "behavior Y" must be excluded (negative).

The first pair of elements indicates an aspect of genuine disciplined living that Jacob hopes to see inculcated into his flock (vv. 19–21a, A). Positively, the followers of Jesus should be characterized by a proclivity to listening, practicing patience and attentiveness to other people, so as to see issues from their perspective. Negatively, the listening attitude will exclude the tendency to ill-considered reflexive (or mindlessly reactive) irritable responses to provocative conversation partners. To listen to others will fortify oneself against angry and aggressive behavior. The parallel statement that closes the paragraph also has a positive and negative component. It urges people to practice others-centered behavior—to care for the marginalized (widows and orphans)[1] who suffer. Again, this

---

1. Care for the marginalized is a major OT theme and central to the understanding of life as God's covenant people. Concern for orphans and widows is abundantly represented in Torah, Prophets, and Writings of the Hebrew Scriptures: see Deut 10:18, 14:29, 24:19–21, 26:13, 27:19; Isa 1:17, 23; Jer 7:6; Ezek 22:7; Mal 3:5; Pss 68:5, 94:6, 146:9.

proactive compassion will have its beneficial consequence. It will have the effect of protecting oneself from conforming to, and being corrupted by, the world (v. 27b, A').[2]

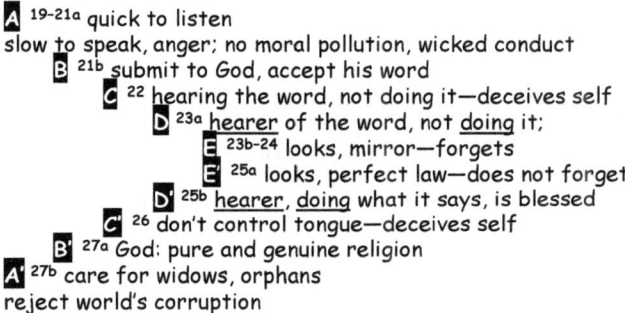

Figure 4. Listening Must Result in Doing

In the second and penultimate elements, the reason for choosing this style of life is given. It is *God* to whom we submit and whose word we obey (v. 21b, B). It is *God* who ordains the nature of pure and authentic religion—that is, a piety uncontaminated by ulterior motives (v. 27a, B'). To the modern mind, *religion* (Greek: *threskeia*) may have different meanings to what it meant to the ancients. To us, religion is a system of belief; to the ancients, it carried the meaning of worship and the fear and love of God.[3] It was an inner disposition, focused on God, a Christlike piety,[4] and Jacob made it clear that it involved charitable acts.[5] In these elements of Jacob's letter, the challenge is to embody true piety, a devotion

---

2. Jacob here refers to *the world* as "the present condition of human affairs, in alienation from and opposition to God"; Vine, *Expository Dictionary*, 233. This meaning was absent from the synoptic gospels but frequent in John's (John 7:7; 8:23; 12:31; 14:17, 27, 30; 15:18, 19; 16:8, 11, 20, 33; 17:14, 16, 25), even though Jacob and the synoptic writers drew from the same reports of Jesus' ethical teaching.

3. Harrison, *Territories*, 8–9.

4. Harrison, *Territories*, 10.

5. Harrison, *Territories*, 35.

that necessarily manifests itself in loving and active compassion for those who are in need.

The next pair of elements develops the theme of practicing what we preach. Jacob warns his readers against self-deception. If we merely listen to God's word without putting it into practice, we *deceive* ourselves (v. 22, C). As a special case of this requirement for moral performance, we must exert control over our spoken words, and if we do not control what we say, we are again *self-deluded* about the reality of our devotion to God (v. 26, C').[6] To Jacob, piety without charity (shown in practice, C, and in a special case, without wholesome speech, C') is a nonsensical state, an oxymoron. He will return to this theme (faith and action, the tangible signs of faith) with some vehemence.[7]

The central elements (D, E) reiterate the importance of listening to (or looking into) God's word and obeying it. We can be *hearers* of God's word without *doing* it (v. 23a, D).[8] Alternatively, we can choose to be *hearers* who take it to heart, and *do* what it commands (v. 25b, D'). "The 'word' in question is the 'perfect law that gives freedom,'"[9] that is elsewhere described as "'the royal law found in Scripture,' 'the whole law,' and 'the law that gives freedom.'" This "law" pertains to the command to love,[10] and so it is concerned with relationships between people, not the adoption of theoretical principles or the performance of symbolic rituals.[11]

When analyzed in this way, the two chiasms of figures 3 and 4 are themselves related. The A elements present defining behavioral characteristics of the faithful believer. The B elements describe how God provides for and blesses those people who are faithful

---

6. Jacob's concern over our speech anticipates 3:1-12 (ch. 7; fig. 7).

7. Jacob's concern over faith and actions (our "doing") anticipates 2:14-26 (ch. 6; fig. 6).

8. The verb *do* (Greek, *poieo*) signifies expressing the mind by means of concrete actions, so indicating a number of terms, "chiefly to make, produce, create, cause" (Vine, *Expository Dictionary*, 330).

9. Jacob 1:25; Wright and Bird, *New Testament*, 741, 743.

10. Lev 19:18.

11. Jacob 2:8, 10, 12; Wright and Bird, *New Testament*, 743.

to him. The C elements list human failings. These are the doubt and concomitant evil desire that destroy moral character; the self-deception that reduces piety to mere sham. The D elements describe people's divergent lifestyles and destinies. There are those who doubt (who receive nothing) and those who are faithful (who receive life); there are those who are not doers and those who are active in their doing (who are blessed). And the central E elements have to do with the people upon whom God's blessing fall: the faithful poor and those who listen attentively and retentively to the divine law of love.

5

PREJUDICE OR LOVE

THE THIRD TOPIC ARISES with a third appeal to the "brothers" and is expressed in a third chiastic structure (2:1–13; fig. 5). It is a sincere warning against prejudice or favoritism: the ever-present tendency to place special value on people whom we might naturally consider particularly attractive—in this case, those who are wealthy.

Like the last homily, the first and last elements have a statement of what Jesus' followers are and what they should take care to reject. Positively, the addressees are people who believe in "our Lord Jesus Christ," and upon whom a moral imperative is placed. Negatively, they are not to give preferential regard (show *prejudice* or *partiality*) to anyone on the basis of superficial criteria such as his or her wealth (v. 1; A). And equally, positively, they are bound to obey the law of God's kingdom, which is to love indiscriminately whilst (negatively) eschewing all *prejudice* or *partiality* (vv. 8–13, A'). To love is the fundamental, all-encompassing requirement of people who would be servants in God's kingdom. Jesus himself said this much.[1] So did

---

1. Mark 12:28–34; Matt 22:34–40; Luke 10:25–28; John 13:34–35; 15:9–10, 12; 17:26. White notes that Jesus quoted Lev 19:18 three times in Matthew's Gospel (5:43; 19:19; 22:39) and he illustrated "love your neighbour" in "innumerable counsels, examples, applications, and commands." Such love is that "active sympathetic imagination, which transfers others' distress to our own hearts, and determines what is right, good, fitting, and desirable for others, not by what they actually do to us but by what we wish they did." White, *Biblical Ethics*, 82.

PREJUDICE OR LOVE

Paul[2] and John.[3] Those who show preferential treatment on the basis of someone's appearance are lawbreakers, and this conclusion holds regardless of how fully they might consider themselves to fulfill other stipulations of the moral law.

For to value people on the basis of external appearances—clothes, wealth, physical attractiveness, skin color—is to reject the fundamental value that characterizes God and the people of God. We must not relativize the *agape* love of which Jesus is the perfect instantiation.

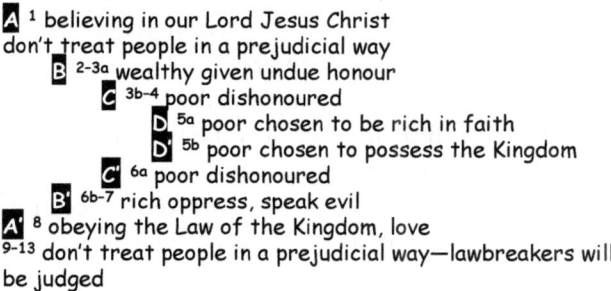

```
A  1 believing in our Lord Jesus Christ
   don't treat people in a prejudicial way
    B  2-3a wealthy given undue honour
     C  3b-4 poor dishonoured
      D  5a poor chosen to be rich in faith
      D  5b poor chosen to possess the Kingdom
     C' 6a poor dishonoured
    B' 6b-7 rich oppress, speak evil
A' 8 obeying the Law of the Kingdom, love
   9-13 don't treat people in a prejudicial way—lawbreakers will
   be judged
```

Figure 5. Prejudice Negates Love

The second and second to last elements focus on those who are wealthy. We are presented with the image of a wealthy man, ostentatiously dressed, and with the possibility of his being given special honor only on the basis of the way he flaunts his baubles of wealth (vv. 2-3a, B). And yet, it is the rich—presumably, the high priestly plutocrats are in Jacob's mind—who have persecuted the believers and who calumniate the name of Jesus, the crucified Messiah, by whom those believers are known (vv. 6b-7, B'). In all of this, the

---

2. Gal 5:13-14; Rom 13:8-10; and Paul teaches the arithmetic of the kingdom of God: $9 - 1 = 0$ (where "9" is a variety of inspiring abilities and gifts, and the "1," of course, is love, the absence of which leaves a person with nothing [1 Cor 13:1-3]).

3. 1 John 3:11-18; 4:7-12, 16-21.

tendency is for people to dishonor the poor—the indigent masses who are of infinite value to God (vv. 3b–4, C; v. 6a, C′).

This homily contains a singular change in those who are censured for prejudicial attitudes. Jacob addresses people *inside* the church who treat the poor with disdain ("you dishonor the poor," [v. 6a]; a little snatch of diatribe) even though they themselves are persecuted believers. He then redirects his ire to those *outside* the church, the rich, who persecute the believers and are hostile to Jesus the Messiah (vv. 6b–7).[4] At face value, it looks as if some of the believers have imported worldly prejudices into the community. The church should be a refuge where everyone finds acceptance. History shows that this ideal has been rejected frequently. The persecuted have often become persecutors.

The central focus of the homily reveals God's concern for the poor. God has chosen them to possess the true riches, that is, to be people of faith (v. 5a, D) and to be valued participants in his kingdom (v. 5b, D′). God's values totally invert those of human society. Jesus made that abundantly clear.[5] But we often overlook the point. Preaching must be backed up by active charity. Perhaps we have forgotten (for example) that the Victorian pastor Charles Spurgeon "made the church the centre of social service," rebuilding houses for the poor, providing free evening schools, loan societies, maternal societies, supporting temperance work, caring for blind people, running Ragged Schools (free education for poor children), supporting Shaftesbury's factory reforms and Barnardo's work for homeless children.[6]

Jacob's warning against prejudice is particularly relevant in our cultural environment of entertainment and social media. The rich, beautiful, and talented (athletes, actors, entertainers) are valued over the rank and file, or as the elite might regard them

---

4. The scenario describes a *wealthy* man who comes into the gathering; the term *rich* (vv. 6b–7; *plousioi*, those who persecute) is reserved for those outside the church; see Davids, "James," in *NBC* 1359–60.

5. Luke 4:18; Matt 11:5 // Luke 7:22.

6. White, *Insights of History*, 276–77; Spurgeon was involved in other initiatives not listed above.

with contempt, the "unwashed masses." In our world, favoritism has reached an extreme form in the unlimited exposure and adulation accorded to celebrities. And many "ordinary" people seek to discover their worth by becoming attractive and apparently happy like their role models. The harmful psychiatric effects of celebrity worship currently constitute a major research concern in the medical literature.[7] Favoritism is incompatible with the values of God's kingdom by denying the God-given value of "ordinary people." It is also frankly harmful to those who indulge in it.

---

7. For example, celebrity worship is related to narcissism (self-love) and a sense of entitlement. See Ash, "Neural Correlates," 1499. Excessive levels of admiration for popular figures are also related to a greater burden of anxiety, depression, and stress, as well as to problematic internet use. See Zsila, "Prevalence," 463–72.

6

FAITH AND ACTIONS

THE PREVIOUS HOMILY ADDRESSED the question of people's *attitudes* to others. The current one addresses *actions* as they impact others (2:14–26). Jacob argues strongly that genuine faith in Jesus is evidenced by corresponding effects on the way people live.[1] A community of faith must manifest the character of the Lord who has gathered the people into that community. The reality of real faith is shown by a Christlike life of love. Authentic faith motivates and flows into compassionate deeds like those of Jesus. We might summarize Jacob's concern about a person's coming to true faith by this maxim: "If there is no obvious outer change in that person's life, it's obvious there is no inner change."

We should first define the genuine faith of which actions are the sign. To Jacob, true faith (as opposed to the mere head-knowledge that he criticizes) means *commitment*.[2] In this, his un-

---

1. The reformer Martin Luther (1483–1546) was concerned to establish that people are put right with God by faith and not by "works," such as acts of penance or almsgiving. He misunderstood Jacob's emphasis on the necessity of "works," described as a holy life motivated by a genuine faith. We will not dwell on this historically located red herring, but see Evans, *Jesus to the Church*, 88–93, or Wright and Bird, *New Testament*, 744–46. In this homily, Jacob may be comparing true active faith with the abstract, rigid orthodoxy of the Pharisees. See Carson, "James," in *IBC* 1541; Kaiser et al., *Hard Sayings*, 696–99.

2. Jacob 1:6 and 2:1; Kaiser et al., *Hard Sayings*, 697.

derstanding of *faith* is derived from that taught by Jesus. The *faith* that people showed when Jesus healed them was "the recognition that Israel's god is active in and through Jesus."[3] It was not simply a belief that Jesus could perform a healing miracle but that "Israel's god is acting climactically in the career of Jesus himself," that here, in Jesus, God's promised kingdom had come.[4] To Paul, faith in Jesus required the triptych of intellectual assent, a daily walk of trust, and a response in obedience. "Biblical faith is never merely something we think; it is also seething we do."[5]

The chiastically structured sermon (fig. 6) starts by raising the questions around the relationship between true faith and actions (vv. 14–18, A). Jacob is aware that alternative understandings have been entertained, but he presents his conviction at this point: his faith is demonstrable *by* his actions. He concludes the homily by restating the necessary connection, that true faith must issue in actions, deeds, lifestyle (v. 26, A′).

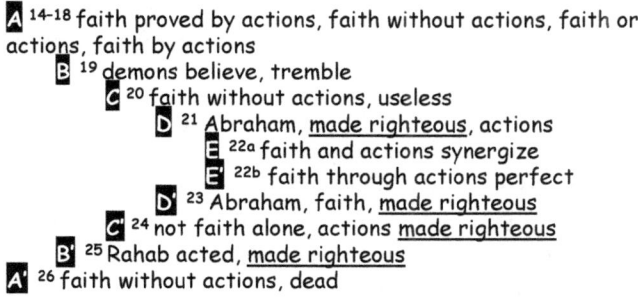

Figure 6. Faith and Actions

In the second and second to last elements, Jacob describes unlovely beings who had divergent destinies because of divergent expressions of "faith." First are the demons, whose variety of "faith" is purely academic (v. 19, B). They recognize the existence of the

3. Wright, *Jesus*, 194.
4. Wright, *Jesus*, 261–63.
5. Bailey, *Jesus*, 258.

one God. The language Jacob uses is akin to the opening utterance of Israel's sacred creed, the Shema, the core of orthodox Jewish faith ("The LORD our God, the LORD is one"), but they do not follow this up with the imperative to love this God.[6] Theirs is a minimally intellectual notion of "belief," one apparently without consequences for their loyalties. This "faith" does not lead to submission to, or an active love for, that one God. They are said to tremble with fear. However we may construe that head-knowledge, it lacks efficacy and therefore reality. It remains merely academic.

On the other hand, at the end of the chiasm (v. 25, B′), we are introduced to another person who scores very poorly on the scale of respectability. Rahab was a woman (a second-class human being in that culture), an idol-worshiper, a Canaanite, a prostitute, and, we might add, one who also trembled in fear at the approach of Israel's God.[7] Her prospects were not bright. But she showed hospitality to Israel's spies (seen as an act of charity),[8] changed sides, and chose to align herself in a demonstrable way with the people of Israel's God. As a result, she was spared the slaughter to come and came to possess a position of honor in the formative history of the Jewish people.[9]

Followers of Jesus do not have a commission to convince people that "God exists." Their responsibility is to show people what *kind* of God exists.[10] Attempts over the years to prove that God exists have been counterproductive. Rather, God is self-revealing and deals with creatures in love and compassion, grace and mercy, righteousness and justice. The *kind* of God who exists is known only through Jesus of Nazareth—the counterintuitive nature of his teaching and acts of healing, the shocking scandal of this death, and the wholly unanticipatable surprise of his resurrection. God

---

6. Deut 6:4–5, NIV; see Davids, "James," in *NBC* 1361; Kaiser et al., *Hard Sayings*, 697.

7. Josh 2; for the terror experienced by the Canaanite people, vv. 9, 11, 24.

8. Kaiser et al., *Hard Sayings*, 697.

9. Josh 6:22–25; Matt 1:6; Heb 11:31.

10. Hauerwas and Willimon, *Resident Aliens*, 95.

calls people to be active disciples who do deeds of love, not who hold forth as passive armchair philosophers.

The "C" elements then stress the conclusion in the most direct language. Any kind of "faith" that lacks telltale actions is void. It is wholly inconsequential (v. 20, C) and lacks any power to put a person right with God. The person who possesses only that abstract "faith" cannot be accepted as righteous before God (v. 24, C').

The central elements feature Abraham, the paradigm of faith-motivated action. And with Abraham comes the key concept of someone's "being made righteous before God" or justified. The mode of how this status arises before God is demonstrated by Abraham's *actions* or *deeds* (v. 21, D). The parallel element states that Abraham was made righteous by this kind of action-evinced faith (v. 23, D'). Jacob thus shares with the other New Testament writers the conviction that it is authentic faith that led to Abraham being called God's friend.[11] This is reinforced by the direct parallel of verse 22 (E, E'). Active faith (or faithful actions) is a synergistic unity that has a concreteness, a dynamism, that is absent from either abstract "faith" or self-directed activism, each understood in isolation.

Jacob has already written of the authentic kind of faith in action. He has urged upon his readers that they practice a faith that, when tested by adversity, produces endurance (1:3). Faith is known by and produces resolute disciplined perseverance.

There is an asymmetrical aspect to this chiasm. The concept of being *made righteous* first appears in the D elements. But it features in the second part of the chiasm, emphasizing how Abraham was made right with God (v. 24, C'), and further developed by the example of Rahab (v. 25, B'). The passive voice indicates that this is the work of God. Such justification is made possible only by God's initiative and grace.

At times, I have found the story of Abraham's willingness to offer Isaac to be distasteful. How could something as sickening as human sacrifice even be mentioned in the Bible? Human sacrifice was widespread among the Canaanites, but God did not allow

---

11. 2 Chr 20:7; Isa 41:8.

Abraham to go ahead with this act of devotion. This story made it clear that the practice was absolutely proscribed, forbidden, among God's covenant people.

The point of the story is that Abraham could step into the darkness (*action*) because he had absolute confidence (*faith*) in God's covenant, *which would be fulfilled only through Isaac and Isaac's descendants*. "I will establish my covenant with [Isaac] as an everlasting covenant for his descendants after him."[12] On the basis of this utterly dependable divine commitment, "Abraham's faith was proved by his willingness to sacrifice Isaac at the apparent demand of God."[13] Abraham was also sure that, when it came to reconciliation of God and humanity, God was the one who would provide the sacrifice.[14]

---

12. Gen 17:19, NIV; and see Yates, "Genesis," in *WBC* 27–28.
13. Barclay, *Letters*, 92.
14. Gen 22:8, 13–14; see Payne, "Genesis," in *IBC* 130.

7

CONTROLLING THE TONGUE

JACOB'S NEXT TOPIC SEEMS to be composed of at least two parts (or homilies), each in chiastic form. The first homily is about the tongue—it is an analysis of the effects of our spoken words (3:1–12; fig. 7). The take-home message is very discouraging. Jacob speaks about the effects of the tongue as being predominantly harmful. It is a wrecking ball, small but possessing a disproportionately large and destructive influence on people. The effect of this homily is to leave the reader feeling deflated—but it raises the question of how people may find alternative and constructive ways of using the tongue. The homily that follows (3:13–18; fig. 8) provides a route out of the human predicament. In the same way that we may opt for true faith over pseudo-faith, we may in our conversation and instruction choose true wisdom (that comes from God) over pseudo-wisdom (that reflects the mores of the unbelieving world).

OUR DESTRUCTIVE TONGUE

Jacob seems to be concerned for teachers in the church. Perhaps they were engaged in rancorous debate.[1] Even teachers are solemnly warned against the injurious potential of the misspoken word. The outermost elements of the tongue homily (fig. 7) reflect

---

1. As suggested by Davids, "James," in *NBC* 1363.

on the difficulty of bringing it under *control* (GNT).² Only if our speech was perfect (which it is not) could we be said to truly control our lives (v. 2, A). The conclusion of the homily is even more uncompromisingly pessimistic: we simply cannot control what we say, and our conversation can be death-dealing, like a viper's poison (vv. 8b–12, A'). Jacob considers how our words can be totally inconsistent in their intended effects. People's words directed towards God may be full of praise, but directed towards other people may be derogatory, offensive, and downright damaging. We can use flowery words to extol God, but this is merely sanctimonious cant when we excoriate others who are created in the likeness[3] of that God (vv. 9–12). Such inconsistency is a contradiction in terms. We are living a lie when we indulge in it.

One implication of our being said to possess the likeness of God is that "we are in a covenantal relationship to God, a relation of trust and responsibility." It follows that, as human beings, "we are related to each other . . . because we are all related to the triune God, creator and redeemer, and are thus responsible to and for each other and the rest of creation."[4] The believer desires that everybody constituting human society would be united and transformed into the image and likeness of the triune God.[5] When we verbally disparage each other, we thereby reject the purpose of our calling to be disciples and we diminish our own humanity.

---

2. Other translations use alternative words to express the sense of *control* (v. 2, A) as opposed to *lack of control* (v. 8, A'): bridle versus unruly (RSV); keep in check versus a restless evil (NIV); control versus a pest that will not keep still (JB); control versus liable to break out (JBP).

3. The reference (v. 9) to people bearing the image/likeness of God is only the fourth time that the term is used in the Bible (Gen 1:26–27, 5:1, 9:6). But the *concept* is pervasive through Scripture, and it underlies the dignity accorded to every person in societies illuminated by the Bible.

4. de Gruchy, *Christianity*, 239.

5. de Gruchy, *Christianity*, 240.

Controlling the Tongue

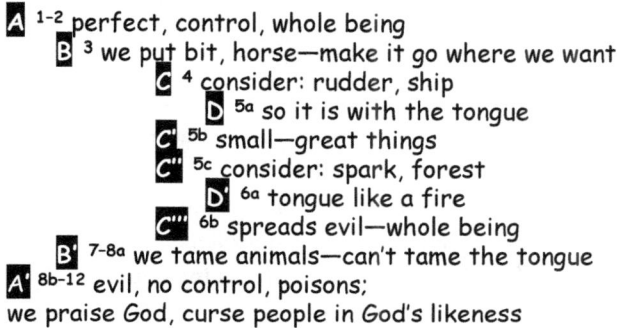

Figure 7. Controlling the Tongue

The second and penultimate elements use analogies from the world of animals to describe the huge and harmful impact of the tongue. A tiny iron bit in the mouth of a horse is used to direct this most powerful of animals that humans have recruited into service (v. 3, B). These imposing creatures first have been broken in, so as to yield to the rider's will for the entire duration of the horse's utility, as mediated through the insignificant-looking bit. This observation is generalized in the parallel element (vv. 7–8a, B′). All sorts of creatures have been tamed to yield to the purposes of their trainers, but that little muscle in our mouths is refractory to all tutelage.

The center of this chiasm is different in form when compared to the other chiasms in Jacob's letter. Two further metaphors are provided and are ordered as direct parallels (vv. 4–5b, C, D, C′; 5c–6b, C″, D′, C‴). In each case, Jacob first seeks to arrest the reader's attention, "Consider!" and presents the metaphor. The first is of a small rudder and a mighty ship driven by mightier winds. The second is of a tiny spark and the massive forest fire that it can ignite. Second, he states the connection: the rudder and spark are analogies of the tongue. We may overlook them because they appear to be miniscule parts of a greater whole. Then third, the relevance of the metaphor is made clear: like the bit and the spark, the tongue is capable of colossal consequences. As we might expect of a parallelism, the second element is the more graphic, more challenging. Our incendiary tongue is ignited by the very fires of hell (v. 6b).

We may note one other property of this homily. It is *structurally* symmetrical, but its content undergoes development from top to bottom. The first half (from A to C′) is cognizant of the problems associated with the misuse of the tongue, but is concerned mainly to show that it is a tiny organ with huge effects. The idea that these effects may be catastrophically harmful is introduced and emphasized through the second half of the chiasm. The tongue sparks devastating conflagrations (C″, D′), spreading evil that affects the entirety of our lives (C‴). It is not tameable (B′). It is evil and the source of curses that have the effects of deadly poison (A′).[6]

Well thanks, Jacob, you are a real cheer germ. Are we fated to go through life leaving behind us a trail of verbally-mediated devastation? In this homily, Jacob may be meditating on the sobering words of Jesus: "For the mouth speaks what the heart is full of,"[7] and this mouth-heart connection provides the basis of divine judgment. Jacob has reflected on whether there are any whose hearts are absolutely pure and who can fully control their tongues. The answer seemed to be "no." Faced with the destructive capacities of the tongue, we need to assess the state of the inner person and what governs the heart and tongue. This is what Jacob turns to next.

CHOOSE WISDOM

How do we relate the little section about true wisdom (3:13–18, fig. 8) to the preceding homily? Plausibly, it is an extension of the previous one about the spoken word.[8] Teachers are entrusted with

---

6. Paul also described our spoken words in bleak terms, implying that our speech provides the criterion of our unrighteousness; see Rom 3:9–18.

7. Matt 12:34 // Luke 6:45, GNT; Jacob's metaphor of knowing a tree by its fruit (3:12) links with Jesus' teaching (Matt 12:33, 35–37 // Luke 6:43–44).

8. Barclay indicates that the section on wisdom starting at 3:13 is indeed a continuation of the section on the tongue. "Here James goes back . . . to

the responsibility of imparting wisdom to their students and will be judged on their performance with particular rigor (3:1–12, fig. 7). But they must teach the wisdom that comes from God, not that of the world as it exists in rebellion against God. Jacob had argued that the qualification of a true teacher must be in control of what is said (fig. 7). In the following section, he continues his address to those who are wise (*sophos*; technically, a teacher) and have understanding (*epistemon*; expert knowledge).[9] Jacob sets out to define the true wisdom, a primary virtue needed by all genuine teachers, and the mindset that must be instilled into their learners.

Jacob now asks (fig. 8) whether there are any who are genuinely wise (v. 13a, A). He concludes the homily by providing essential characteristics of those who are wise—which may serve as a definition, as wisdom may be defined by its outcomes. The wise are those who work for peace, who invest their energies in producing a harvest (*karpos*, the fruit) of righteousness (v. 18, A′).[10] There may be echoes here of Jesus' beatitude: "Blessed are the peacemakers for they will be called sons of God."[11] Peacemaking is surely the antithesis of the hostility-promoting use of the tongue considered in the previous section. It is a required qualification of any who would serve in the church of Jesus.

---

the beginning of the chapter. His argument runs like this: 'Is there any of you who wishes to be a real sage and a real teacher? Then let him live a life of such beautiful graciousness that he will prove to all that gentleness is enthroned as the controlling power within his heart'" (*Letters*, 106). Davids seems to agree, suggesting that in churches that Jacob knew, teachers were attacking each other. God's wisdom alone was the appropriate alternative for the angry debates ("James" in *NBC* 1363).

9. Jacob 3:13; See Wessel, "James," in *WBC* 1436.

10. In describing an assured "harvest of righteousness" (literally, fruits, *karpon*; 3:17, 18), Jacob may be referring back to the wholly incongruous harvests of the tongue: olives from fig trees, figs from grapevines (3:12).

11. Matt 5:9; see Davids, "James," in *NBC* 1364.

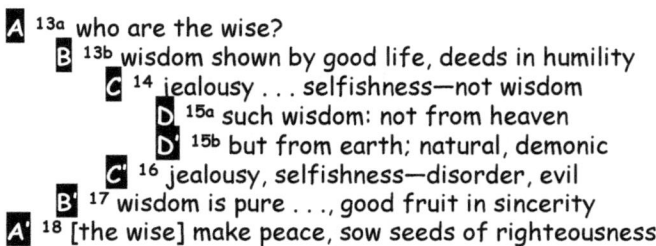

Figure 8. True Wisdom

In the next elements, Jacob elaborates on the visible outcomes, the fruit (we are back into agriculture) of true wisdom. Jacob's list reads like St. Paul's fruit of the Spirit.[12] There must be a good life, good deeds performed in a spirit of humility (v. 13b, B). The parallel element expands on this basic principle by listing a wealth of spiritual virtues. The translation of some of these appears to be challenging, given the variety of English words used in different versions. Genuine wisdom is pure, peaceable, gentle (considerate, kindly), friendly (submissive, open to reason, approachable), and full of mercy (compassionate, tolerant). True wisdom generates the fruit (*karpon*) of good deeds, free from prejudice (impartial, without favoritism) and hypocrisy (insincerity) (v. 17, B'). Just as actions show the reality of someone's faith, so good deeds show the reality of wisdom.

The outputs arising from the worldly type of wisdom are given for comparison in the C elements. Some of the teachers of whom Jacob has heard were showing a selfish ambition that was intransigent and divisive.[13] Barclay described this wrong kind of teaching as fanatical, bitter (preferring annihilation of enemies rather than winsome persuasion), selfishly ambitious (seeking to establish one's own opinions rather than truth), and arrogant.[14] Common to verse 14 (C) and verse 16 (C') are jealousy and

---

12. Gal 5:22–23; see Davids, "James," in *NBC* 1363.
13. See Davids, "James," in *NBC* 1363.
14. Barclay, *Letters*, 108.

selfishness, all too often markers of the academic world of rivalry and one-upmanship. Acrimonious competition for recognition or prestige should not occur in communities of people that bear Jesus' name.[15]

The central elements cut to the chase. There are two ways of possessing what might be called "wisdom." On the one hand, people can pursue the wisdom of heaven—wisdom that has its origin in God (v. 15a, D). Alternatively, people may settle for wisdom from the earth that reflects our human nature and is demonic (v. 15b, D'). We might speak of someone as being "worldly wise" with quasi-comic associations, such as one might see in a wise-cracking smart aleck, a sophisticate, a know-all. But pertinent to Jacob's concerns, there is the sort of wisdom that emerges from the values of earth, from our own "animal" nature (JB). They are the values elsewhere attributed to the world, identified as human society in violent rebellion against God (see 1:27) and are altogether more sinister. This type of false wisdom is described here as demonic. We can recognize this wisdom as originating from hell itself (previous homily, v. 3:6b). It is the dog-eat-dog "wisdom" shown by people fighting each other to get to the top.

In summary, what comes naturally to us, the expression of human wisdom, results in chaos—the very social convulsions we see all around us. The source of true wisdom transcends human nature and intellect. Its practice fosters peace and harmonious relationships. The outcome is a satisfying harvest of righteousness and justice.

---

15. St. Paul had to contend with this same problem; 1 Cor 1:10–17 (where words of human wisdom again prevail); 2 Cor 10:1—11:15; Phil 3:18–19.

8

MORE ON TRUE WISDOM

THE NEXT FOUR SUGGESTED chiasms sound like reprimands. They have the air of a law court about them. The word "you" is used extensively in an accusative manner. *You* are fighting among yourselves (4:1–10). *You* are judging each other (4:11–12). *You* are making plans in an arrogant way (4:13–17). *You* rich people have exploited the helpless poor (5:1–6). Three of the four lack the affectionate introductory address, "my brothers."

To whom is Jacob addressing his censure? Factions feuding in his flock? Or a hypothetical group in danger of patterning their ethics on the evils of the surrounding culture (the "world") from which they have been called? The first three mini-chiasms may be united by the continuing theme of the misuse of the tongue, and the adoption of worldly wisdom.

In the case of the fourth brief homily, Jacob may be arraigning the autocratic high priestly junta as the objects of his censure. But would the high priests be likely to read what Jacob had written in his letter to scattered believers? Possibly not—but his denunciation of the ruthless rich and the promise of divine judgment upon them would bring comfort to the refugees who had been treated harshly and unjustly by their power- and money-hungry rulers.

In any case, if Jacob's letter is a compendium of his sermons, the fourth homily may give an indication of how Jacob repeatedly and outspokenly denounced the rich and powerful—the landowner barons constituting the Jewish council (Sanhedrin)—for their abuses of the innocent and helpless. This gives us an idea of how Jacob's warnings might have been patterned on those of Jesus and how much the despotic leaders must have hated Jacob. He had the reputation of being an ascetic who was deeply devoted to God and prayed continually for the city of Jerusalem. As such, he was greatly respected by the populace at large, but when the opportunity arose, the high priest had Jacob killed by stoning. The year of his death is known to be AD 62.[1]

YOUR QUARRELS

Section 4:1–10 is possibly a chiasm, and the scheme below is given with some tentativeness (fig. 9). It has been suggested that this homily is a response to heated arguments in communities of Jesus' followers.[2]

Jacob's opening salvo seems to indicate that such disagreements were widespread. He addresses the ongoing squabbles that have disrupted the fellowship (v. 1a, A). He concludes the homily with the solution to this divisiveness. Our cantankerous behavior can be overcome only when we take the difficult step of humbling ourselves before God (v. 10, A'). "What?" we might say, "Is this unhappiness really *my* fault?" And the seemingly unpalatable answer is "Yes! Now apologize to, and be reconciled with, that guy you have considered to be an opinionated jerk!" And counterintuitively, if we are prepared to lose face in that way, God will lift us up—*exalt* us (as in 1:9).

---

1. According to the contemporary historian Josephus, the high priest Annas II (the son of Annas I, who, through his own agency and that of his family, dominated Jewish politics for sixty years and was complicit in Jesus' crucifixion) took his opportunity to kill Jacob after the Roman governor Festus died (known to be AD 62) and before Albinus arrived to replace him (that same year). See Josephus, *Antiquities* 20.9.1, in Whiston, *Complete Works*, 656; Bruce, *Israel*, 216; Evans, *Jesus to the Church*, 108–11.

2. See Davids, "James," in *NBC* 1364.

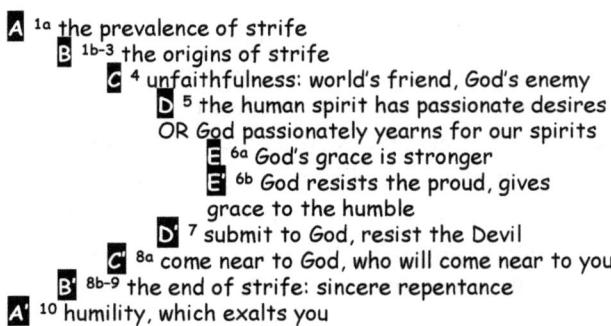

Figure 9. Your Quarrels

The origins of, and solution to, this divisiveness are considered in the following pair of elements. People have an insatiable appetite for self-gratification (vv. 1b–3, B). This leads them to character assassination ("killing with words").[3] The will of God is forgotten in the quest for self-gratification. The desired termination of the strife is to be found only in sincere remorse ("mourn") and repentance ("purify your hearts") (vv. 8b–9, B′).

The following elements relate the selfish and acquisitive evil of the human psyche to its position relative to God. All this strife is a sign that God has been abandoned and people's loyalty transferred to the rebellion (the "world"; see 1:27 and 3:15 above) (v. 4, C). There is no middle ground in this question of commitments, and only one means of remediation is available to us. As we have become estranged from God, so we need to return. We will find that God is waiting to actively come to us in reconciliation (v. 8a, C′).[4]

There is a problem with this homily in that there seems to be no scholarly consensus as to the meaning of v. 5 (D). Its meaning is ambiguous. Different translations indicate at least four alternative meanings, as discussed below, and summarized in table 4.

---

3. See Davids, "James," in *NBC* 1364.

4. Echoes of the parable of the prodigal son trudging home as his father flies to welcome him; Luke 15:11–32.

First, perhaps reflecting the message of the previous elements, it is the *human* spirit, created by God, that is filled with passionate and selfish desires (first alternative, v. 5, D). We could call these perverted motivations lust, and they are the substrate out of which human conflict arises. This interpretation seems to be appropriate for the context, for the next element in the chiasm states that God's grace is *greater*. But greater than what? Surely divine grace is greater than the sin that is present in the human spirit. God's grace *more* than expunges the effects of human evil. It endows upon selfish creatures not only forgiveness but also the gift of God's Spirit, the life of the age to come, and elevation into the very fellowship of God.[5]

Second, it is *God* who has passionate desires for us, his rebellious creatures (second option). God has created our spirits, giving them freedom to choose right or wrong, and God yearns jealously that they (our spirits) will be devoted to him. In this context, *jealously* is used in a wholesome sense—as when parents are jealous for the wellbeing of their children.[6] God is rightly jealous for our misguided spirits, that they will be reorientated, realigned towards the divine holiness.

Third, the Spirit that yearns jealously is that of God, infused into us, his creatures. It is this Holy Spirit that yearns with righteous passion for us to be dedicated to God alone.

Fourth, the statement is a rhetorical question. Is it possible that the Holy Spirit of God is responsible for the passionate desires that foment human strife? The answer clearly is "no." When we are fighting with each other, we cannot claim that God's Spirit is controlling our relationships. Rather, we must examine ourselves. Selfish human nature is exerting its divisive and damaging effects, directing the courses of our lives.

---

5. "Where sin increased, grace increased much more" (Rom 5:20–21).

6. God is jealous for our obedience, which is so central to our well-being (Exod 20:5, 34:14; Deut 5:9; 32:16, 21; Zech 8:2). "God loves men with such a passion that He cannot bear any rival love within the hearts of men" (Barclay, *Letters*, 122–23).

Table 4. Understanding Verse 4:5 (D)

Whose spirit?	Whose desires?	Whose "jealousy"?	Translation
ours	ours	sinful passions	GNT, NIV
ours	God's	holy desire	GNT, NIV footnotes, RSV
God's	God's	holy desire	JB
God's	ours	sinful passions*	JBP

*Rhetorical question: the answer is, "No, God's Spirit is not responsible for our passions."

Analysis of the chiasm may help us resolve this perplexity. The first three elements of the chiasm describe the course of human evil. There are fights and quarrels (A), originating from human lust or idolatry (B), which make us rebels and enemies of God (C). Leaving aside the problematic element (D) for the moment, we find that the last four elements describe the new orientation that God brings in achieving reconciliation. The pivot in the whole argument is the grace of God (E, E'). In order to receive God's grace, we need to submit (D'), come near to God (C'), repent in brokenness of spirit (B'), and humble ourselves so that we may be exalted (A'). It appears that the last four elements (reconciliation with God) are mirror images of the first four (estrangement from God). In this case, the element D must refer to our uncontrolled spirits, madly seeking self-gratification, driving all kinds of selfishness,[7] in contrast to health-giving submission to God (D'). Ultimate responsibility for our conflicted state lies with God because God has created us with the capacity to choose good or evil. We have freely chosen the latter. The one realistic response, the shining alternative to this destructive behavior, is to submit to God (v. 7, D').

---

7. The "envy" of the spirit (v. 5) does seem to belong to the quarrels, fights, covetousness, illicit desires for pleasure, and unfaithfulness of the *human* spirit, as described in the first half of the chiasm.

More on True Wisdom

Suffice it to say the power that transforms selfish and estranged people into restored and reconciled people is God's grace (v. 6, E, E'). This grace is available to everyone who is entrapped by the destructive energies of human violence (A to D) but can be effective only in those who sincerely humble themselves before God (D' to A').

This is a powerful little homily. It may appear to become more incisive the more we progress in the Christian life. It shows us the appalling depths of our sin, the wonder of God's all-sufficient grace, and the need of the profound repentance that allows grace to overwhelm sin.

YOUR CRITICISMS

Two possible mini-chiasms follow. I will leave it to the reader to assess whether the text naturally falls into a chiastic shape or has been forced into one. First, Jacob continues his reflections on the tongue (figs. 7 and 8) by transitioning from *quarrelling* (fig. 9) to *criticizing* (4:11–12; fig. 10). The latter vice seems to indicate malicious gossip, character assassination, backbiting[8]—any critical words that hurt the community by bad-mouthing its members.[9]

```
A  11a do not criticize one another, my brothers
   B  11b to criticize, judge another criticizes, judges the Law
      C  11c if you judge the Law
         D  11d you no longer obey the Law
      C' 11e but judge it
   B' 12a God is the only lawgiver and judge
A' 12b who are you, to judge your neighbour?
```

Figure 10. Your Criticisms

The first and last elements raise the issue of criticism and its absolute inappropriateness in the church community. Jacob introduces the topic with a simple imperative. Do not indulge in

---

8. Barclay, *Letters*, 130.
9. See Davids, "James," in *NBC* 1365.

unkind criticism (v. 11a, A). He concludes it with a trenchant rhetorical question (v. 12b, A′). Who do you think you are to stand over your fellows in judgment, to presume the right to pull the other person down, to arrogate to oneself the authority to interpret the law? The clear implication is that people have no such right to stand over God's law and, moreover, to do so is sheer pride. The law as understood here is presumably the supreme law of love for one's neighbor (2:8). People breach the royal law by judging, not loving, that neighbor (v. 12b, A′).[10]

The next pair of elements considers the source of the law's authority. To pass opinions on other people indicates that we have set ourselves up as the judicial authority. We consider ourselves to be the ones who may rightly interpret what it means. (v. 11b, B). The parallel statement identifies God as the sole source of the law and the only one who can judge people for their fidelity to its requirements (v. 12a, B′).

The C elements reiterate the implications of criticizing others: it is to judge the law, to put ourselves above it, and to modify its requirements according to our own selfish preferences. To put ourselves above the law is to become lawbreakers. We have already come across the principle that people might be punctilious in obeying the law except for one stipulation, the rejection of which is sufficient to make them lawbreakers (2:10–11). Anyone who stands over the law of God has that law in contempt (v. 11d, D).

Jacob's terminology changes as the chiasm develops. What starts as *criticism* (or *slander, speaking against* someone; three times in A and B) morphs into the weightier term *judging* (five times in B to A′). What we might consider to be inconsequential misuse of the tongue turns out to be an indictable offense before God.

But what does it mean to *judge*? It is necessary that we discriminate between right and wrong actions. When does rightful discernment slide into opinionated dismissal or slander of other people's actions, opinions, or motivations? God's law is given to regulate relationships between people and with God, to promote and inspire the expression of love. To use God's law as an excuse

---

10. Barclay, *Letters*, 131.

or justification for denouncing or condemning our fellows is to reimagine it, repurpose it, to reverse its intentions. To so stand in judgment of the law usurps God's authority. We might consider (potentially hurtful) assessments of other people's purposes or activities to be minor infelicities of the tongue, but here they are robustly condemned.

YOUR BOASTING

Just as their human appetites and passions can lead people into conflict with their fellows and with God (fig. 9), and hypercritical mindsets can lead them to pass judgment on other people and on God's own law (fig. 10), so people's quest for independence can lead them to *boastfully* exclude God from their plans (fig. 11). Jacob now turns his attention to a third misuse of the tongue. It is to assert our own autonomy, to overconfidently, brashly, arrogantly determine our aspirations and goals without reference to God. We have tendencies not only to trash others but to extol ourselves.

Jacob first addresses the entrepreneurs who confidently announce their schedules, their destinations, their plans, and their worldly ambitions (v. 13, A). In all of this, there is no reference to God or to what God might desire of an aspiring businessperson. Here are echoes of Jesus' admonition to people preoccupied with food and clothes: "Give first place to the kingdom of God."[11] Only then will the complexities of life resolve into their rightful places. The homily concludes with the warning that to pursue our own ambitions is to repudiate the fundamental requirement of a disciple of Jesus, which is to search for, and do, God's purposes. Jacob's Christian merchants know very well that they should pursue their occupation in a spirit of humble dependence on God. "To *know* this and not to *do* it is sin."[12] Willful autonomy is culpable wrongdoing (v. 17; A'), and so-called disciples (read: *we*) seem to be guilty of it habitually.

---

11. Matt 6:33.
12. See Wessel, "James," in *WBC* 1438.

In these outer parallel elements, a key word seems to relate to people's *doing*. It concerns what they in their pride have set their hearts on *doing* (A), which means that what they *should be doing* (A') is neglected. The definitive statement about what disciples should be doing is provided in the central element.

<pre>
A ¹³ listen, you that say "Today or tomorrow we will travel to
a certain city, stay a year, do business, make money"
   B ¹⁴ᵃ you don't know what your life tomorrow will be
      C ¹⁴ᵇ you are like a puff of smoke, momentary,
      disappearing
         D ¹⁵ᵃ you should say "If the Lord is willing, we
         will live
         D' ¹⁵ᵇ and do this or that"
      C' ¹⁶ᵃ now you are proud
   B' ¹⁶ᵇ you boast; all such boasting is wrong
A' ¹⁷ if we do not do the good we know we should do, we are
guilty of sin
</pre>

Figure 11. Your Boasting

In the second and penultimate elements, Jacob's readers are reminded of the incongruity of such presumptuous behavior. They cannot anticipate even the immediate future (v. 14a, B). Any such confident prognostications bely people's ignorance, their lack of foresight or control over what may soon eventuate. To utter such predictions is to indulge in foolish bragging (v. 16b, B').

The intensity of the argument increases in the next pair of elements. The continuation of our very lives, not merely our plans, cannot be guaranteed. Our lives are ephemeral, dreamlike, transient (v. 14b, C). Given our tenuous hold on life, any talk of self-determination is simply overweening pride (v. 16a, C').

The focus of the homily is what we know to be true, but conveniently forget. We are utterly dependent upon God for our very lives, moment by moment, and for everything we might hope to achieve in them (v. 15a, D). And the second part of the "hinge" provides the answer to the question of what we should do (as raised in A, A'). We should continuously seek out and practice (*do*) the will of God (v. 15b, D'). This is inherent to being a disciple.

In those times when we live most fully for each instant of time (whether through the heightened awareness that we may receive through pain or sickness, joyful or difficult circumstance), our dependence on our heavenly Father is most immediately palpable. The reality of the present moment is that infinitely fine interface between the remembered, unchangeable past and the hypothetical, uncontrollable future.[13] God must be determinative of our thoughts and actions in that ever-moving instant of concrete reality. It is in the timeless present when we meet and respond to God in God's eternity.

We have noted before (figs. 6, 7) that chiasms have a structural symmetry, but there may be a development of thought from beginning to end. That seems to be true of this homily also. The first elements A, B, and C describe human plans in all their weakness, fallibility, and illusionary nature. D is the hinge, pivot. It provides the spiritual insight and moral imperative that challenge us to live according to an authentically Christian outlook. Then C′, B′, and A′ deal with our misplaced self-confidence that is in fact pride, which is thus boastful, totally wrongheaded, and ultimately sinful.

We live in a world in which there is an ever-increasing tendency to make decisions without any reference to God. Indeed, the ultimate virtue is thought to be unlimited freedom. David Bentley Hart has said that the contemporary notion of *freedom* is found primarily "in an individual subject's spontaneous power of choice, rather than in the ends that subject may actually choose." Freedom is now considered to be the power to choose whatever people want. "Neither God, then, nor nature, nor reason provides the measure of an act's true liberty."[14] Concomitantly, there seems to be increasing concern over unhappiness, crime, depression, fear, and mental illness. The exercise of radical autonomy must have its disastrous consequences.

Those who claim to follow Jesus still have a window of opportunity to bring healing to this world if, in humility, they will

---

13. An insight from professor Andrew Gosler, "Hearing God," in Alexander, *Coming*, 115–17.

14. Hart, *Atheist Delusions*, 224.

A Letter to Stressed Communities

seek to know and do the will of God. As Peter wrote, to live as free people is to live as God's slaves.[15]

YOUR EXPLOITATION

This homily (fig. 12) represents a break with all those that have preceded it in Jacob's letter. It is a direct challenge to, indeed a condemnation of, people outside the church. Jacob here arraigns the ruling class for their misuse of power. It is hardly surprising that it was their chief Annas II who was to have Jacob murdered.

The outermost elements directly challenge the rich, understood as the powerful oligarchs who comprise the Sanhedrin, the seat of Jewish power, and who killed Jesus and subsequently persecuted his followers.[16] The tone is an uncompromising prophetic denunciation. These despotic rulers were warned of judgment bearing down on them (v. 1, A). And the offense for which they were charged was their own egregious injustice meted out upon helpless people who had done no wrong (v. 6, A').

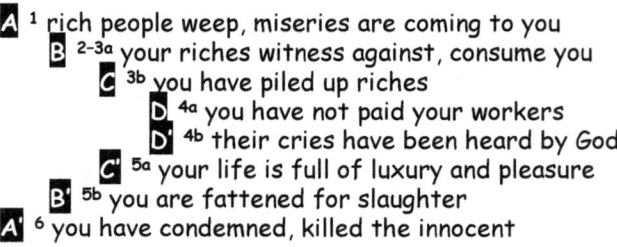

Figure 12. Your Exploitation

The rapacious rich had accumulated great wealth, which was supposed to give them protection against the vicissitudes of life. But such riches could not buffer them against the horrors to come. Jacob echoes the teaching of Jesus regarding the misguided priority

---

15. 1 Peter 2:16.
16. As corroborated by St. Paul, 1 Thess 2:14–15.

of seeking security in riches. Riches will ultimately be lost by rust, rot, or robbery. This was not a bright prospect as people's hearts, their deepest loyalties, would always be where their riches are.[17] Jacob argued that the unjustly acquired wealth of the rich would act like a witness in a law court. It would testify to their ruthless avarice. And far from keeping them well nourished and sleek, their wealth would destroy their lives in the same way as a spreading ulcer or gangrenous lesion destroys human flesh (vv. 2–3a, B). The weight of their possessions would not guarantee health and ease in the future but would bring them to an early and violent death (v. 5b, B'). Was Jacob offering these warnings with the precedents of history in mind, or was he seeing seething resentments, signs portending revolution?[18]

The charge against the rich is repeated succinctly in the third and third from last elements (vv. 3b, C; 5a, C'). It seems that the rich were being condemned not only for the *means* of acquiring their possessions but also for the grossly excessive *accumulation* of their possessions and the way they supported lifestyles that were *extravagantly hedonistic*. The ancients recognized that resources were limited, so that what was possessed by the wealthy was not available to the poor. This understanding had been forgotten but is now recovered by ecologists.[19] Both the hoarding and the self-indulgent use of wealth are hereby condemned—not merely the ruthless actions by which it is acquired.

---

17. Matt 6:19–21; and see the parable of the rich fool, Luke 12:13–21.

18. One of the plutocratic high priestly dynasty, Jonathan son of Annas ("John" of Acts 4:6?) was assassinated by the *sicarii* ("dagger men") as the Jewish revolution (AD 66–70) approached. See Josephus, *Antiquities* 20.8.5, in Whiston, *Complete Works*, 653; *Jewish War* 2.13.3, in *Complete Works*, 747. Another member of the high priestly cohort, Annas II, who had Jacob murdered in AD 62, was himself killed (in 68 or thereabouts) on suspicion of being ready to negotiate with the Romans. See Josephus, *Jewish War* 4.5.2, in Whiston, *Complete Works*, 822. The last high priest of the family, Matthias ben Theophilus, with three of his sons, was killed by the revolutionary Simon bar Giora. See Josephus, *Jewish War* 6.2.2, in Whiston, *Complete Works*, 887; Bruce, *Israel*, 214, 222, 235.

19. Kaiser et al., *Hard Sayings*, 703.

A Letter to Stressed Communities

The focus of the homily considers those who have been exploited. They have not been paid for their labor (v. 4a, D).[20] They have called out to God for redress. And God has taken note of their predicament (v. 4b, D'). Exploitation of workers is as old as human history. But divine judgment on those who indulge in such evil practices is certain. What is less certain is that Christian communities will follow Jacob's example in advocating for and acting on behalf of the downtrodden poor. In an age when there are vast disparities in spending power, Christians have a divinely-given obligation to be committed to showing compassion and practical care for the many people who have been denied the resources needed for an adequate lifestyle.

---

20. Prompt payment for labor was required in the Law of Moses (Lev 19:13; Deut 24:14–15) and was the mark of a righteousness man (Job 31:39), but all too often, this commandment had been ignored through Israel's history (Jer 22:13; Mal 3:5); see Davids, "James," in *NBC* 1366; Kaiser et al., *Hard Sayings*, 702–3.

9

COMMUNITY HEALTH

Patience, Integrity, Prayer

AT FIRST GLANCE, THE last section of Jacob's letter seems to be a mixed ramble. It is introduced by the appeal to "my brothers," which is diagnostic of the major chiasms. And a plausible case can be made that, structurally, it falls into a recognizable chiasm (fig. 13). However, the first four elements (A to D) feature patience and the last four (D' to A') constitute an appeal to faithful prayer. The hinge seems to be the climax, as it is prefixed by "above all" with "my brothers" thrown in for effect (E, E'). This conceptual center is about truth-speaking. This homily seems to necessitate that there is a relationship between patience, truth-telling, and prayer. Or are we dealing here with a chiastic unit constituted by a series of nonsequiturs?

Closer reflection suggests that a common theme of these disparate elements is that they all have to do with fostering unity in the community. And unity underlies health. The homily presents its readers with a choice between integration or disintegration. Evidence for the chiasm being a single unit comes from the similarity of the C elements (and their relationship to the central focus). First, an important outcome of *patience* is that it precludes complaining or grumbling against other members of the group (v. 9a, C). Patience is a property that has a pacifying, health-promoting effect.

Second, an important part of *prayer* is that we are confronted with our own sin and focused on the wellbeing of each other. This must generate humility and empathy for others. Indeed, prayer for each other is said to be healing (v. 16, C′).[1] In the center of this other-orientated ethos ("above all") is the supreme value of transparent honesty (v. 12, E, E′). This gives no occasion for the manipulation of others or for generating social environments poisoned by ruinous suspicion.

It seems that this last chiasm is a concluding appeal to the community to practice what is unifying. There is a trio of patience (engendering serenity), absolute integrity (fostering trust), and prayer (issuing in healing). Jacob has brought us back to considering the tongue but, in this case, its constructive use. And patience, truth-telling, and prayer all contribute to the strengthening of relationships in the community.[2]

Given this suggested overview, we may work our way through the paragraph. The importance of patience in the first element (v. 7, A) and of prayer in the last (vv. 17–18, A′) is emphasized. These elements use the same metaphor: people wait patiently (or pray) for the rain that is essential for the earth to bring forth its precious fruit (*karpon*, vv. 7, 18). This is a powerful metaphor in a land that is inherently water-stressed. Rain is life-giving. In our spiritual lives, this agricultural image enjoins us to patience and to earnest prayer while we await growth into Christlikeness.

---

1. Confession and health are connected: "It would be better to take care of sin before it causes severe illness. *Confess your sins to each other.*" See Davids, "James," in *NBC* 1367.

2. Interestingly, this chiastically defined homily seems to be composed of two separate chiasms, one focused on patience, the other on prayer. These component chiasms are presented in appendix 2.

COMMUNITY HEALTH

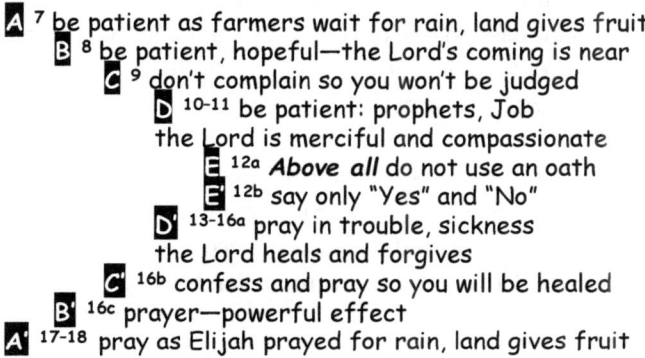

Figure 13. Patience, Integrity, Prayer: Health in the Community

The second (v. 8, B) and second to last (v. 16c, B') elements restate these exhortations simply and directly. The members of the community are urged to practice patience (whilst keeping their hopes high). And they must pray for each other (whilst expecting those prayers to be effective).

Consequences of adopting such virtues follow in the next pair of strongly paralleled statements. Don't complain *against one another, so that you will* not come under God's judgment (v. 9, C); do confess your sin *to one another* and pray *for one another, so that you will* be healed (v. 16b, C'). These elements consider how the believers relate to each other and describe the healthful, beneficial outcomes of that pursuit of intimacy in relationship. To model patience (faith under duress, fig. 3) is to place oneself beyond the circle of God's judgment. It is a mindset that excludes implosion into self-pity or explosion in rage. To confess sin and pray is to allow God's healing power to operate in our lives.

Each of the D elements has two parts. Each repeats the benefits of patience and prayer, providing examples of those who illustrate this. And these exhortations are undergirded by the goodness of the Lord. Paradigms of patience are encountered in the persecuted prophets[3] and in the figure of Job, who had to bear many

---

3. Matt 23:29-36 // Luke 11:47-51; see the fates of the servants (prophets)

61

types of afflictions. Their patience was vindicated because of God's mercy and compassion (vv. 10–11, D). For those in trouble or sickness, there should be prayer that includes confession. Restoration to health follows because of God's commitment to heal and forgive (vv. 13–16a, D').[4]

The healing process seems to involve three results flowing from confession of wrongdoing. First, confession is required for divine forgiveness. Second, it leads to reconciliation with other people. Third, it may be a prerequisite for healing.[5] Wright and Bird comment that

> members of the community must confess their sins to one another and pray for healing in their bodies and souls . . . the person praying stands with one foot in the place of trouble, sickness, and sin, and with the other foot in the place of healing, forgiveness, and hope.[6]

The central focus has a similar structure to that of the C elements. Always speak the truth without allowing degrees of commitment (v. 12a, E), *so that you will* not come under God's judgment (v. 12b, E'). There should be no wriggle room when it comes to commitments made. This stands in blazing contradistinction to the post-truth age into which society has fallen.

In summary, the chiasm is a single homiletic unit that shows the way to peace and health or wholeness. Jacob might have stated (if he wrote in Hebrew) that these are properties which constitute the rich sense of *shalom*. This broad concept referred to "the healing and wholeness of human relationships," as well as the wellbeing

---

in the parable of the tenanted vineyard (Mark 12:1–12 // Matt 21:33–46 // Luke 20:9–18).

4. "This is not to suggest that God always answers believing prayer. All prayer, including prayer for healing, is subject to the will of God. Sometimes, certainly not always, sickness is the result of personal sin. Perhaps this is what is meant by 'if he has committed sins'" (Wessel, "James," in *WBC* 1439).

5. "All sickness does not have to do with sin (John 9:3), but sin can cause sickness (1 Cor. 11:30). If sin is involved, then this root needs to be dealt with before moving on to the fruit of the root, the sickness itself" (Davids, "James," in *NBC* 1367).

6. Wright and Bird, *New Testament*, 748.

of creation and the covenant relationship between God and the people. It included the idea of salvation and presupposed the doing of justice.[7] "The Church has always cared for her sick; and in the Church there has always resided the gift of healing. The social gospel is not an appendix to Christianity; it is the very essence of Christian faith and life."[8] It is another case of authentic faith issuing in concrete actions.

---

7. de Gruchy, *Christianity*, 44.
8. Barclay, *James*, 153.

10

SUMMING UP

JACOB CHALLENGES HIS READERS with straight talk. They are faced with starkly dichotomous choices. Everyone must choose how they will live. There are the faithful poor and the oppressing rich. Some people read God's law and do not forget about it, whereas others simply ignore it. Some have a productive, vibrant faith and others a sterile, dead orthodoxy that falls short of true faith. People adopt either wisdom that comes from God or a pseudo-wisdom that belongs to the world. They may opt for passionate selfishness or humble repentance. Our outlook may be humble or arrogant. We may be obedient to the law of love or stand in judgment over it; act in accordance with God's will or with our own; show simple "yes or no" integrity or intend to practice various degrees of "truthfulness."

In this call for right moral decision, Jacob's letter is very much like part 1 of the Didache, a manual of Christian ethics probably dating from later in the first century: "There are two Ways: a Way of Life and a Way of Death, and the difference between these two Ways is great."[1] One might add that to travel by the Way of Life is to be true disciples, and the other way can be chosen simply by being fence-sitters—as Jacob calls them, *dipsuchos* (two-souled; 1:8; 4:8), unable to make up their minds or hypocritical (GNT),

---

1. Louth, *Early Christian Writings*, 227 (the text of part 1 of the Didache is given in pp. 227–30).

double-minded (NIV), wavering between going different ways (JB).

Jacob's letter is a clear reflection of the teaching of Jesus, which to human sensitivities is deeply paradoxical. The values generally accepted in human society (the "world") are inverted—turned upside down—by Jesus and by Jacob. So strangely, counterintuitively, the fortunate people are those who go through trials (1:2). Those called happy are the ones who have endured sufferings (5:11). The people who should be glad are the anonymous poor (1:9) because they are rich in faith (2:5). The best that can happen to the rich is for them to recognize the emptiness of their opulent condition (1:10), because the extravagant and dominating lifestyle in which they have placed their hope will lead to destruction (1:11), miseries (5:1), even to annihilation (5:5).

Jacob adds two beatitudes to those of Jesus. The person is blessed, happy, truly fortunate, who remains faithful or who endures under trials (1:12; 5:11). The person is blessed who puts God's law into practice (1:25). These values again break with society's received wisdom.

If the central element(s) of each chiasm embodies its conceptual focus, and if Jacob intends to propagate the ethics of Jesus, then each such "hinge" should have rich associations with the teachings of Jesus as reported in the Gospels. This seems to be so, and some allusions are indicated in table 5. The central focus of each chiasm may strongly parallel (chiasms 1, 3, 6, diatribe 3), extend (chiasm 4, diatribe 1) or otherwise echo (chiasms 2, 5a, 5b, diatribes 2, 4) what Jesus had to say about life in the kingdom of God.

For example, in homily 1, the enviable position of the poor, who are exalted by God, and the rich, who are humbled, reflects Jesus' otherworldly wisdom that the poor are blessed and the greatest are those who humble themselves. Jacob's depiction of the rich man fading away in the midst of his business (1:10) resonates with the parable of the rich fool,[2] and perhaps with the parable of Lazarus and the beggar, and with Jesus' warning that the rich enter the kingdom of God only with great difficulty.

---

2. Luke 12:13–31; Bailey, *Jesus*, 308.

Some people have suggested that Jacob's letter is lightweight when it comes to theological themes. Against this, the "hinge" of chiasm 4 emphasized the great theme of *faith*, probably understood as committed belief that Jesus' career represents the return of God to Israel in order to complete God's eschatological purposes. Jacob's treatment of faith reflects Jesus' pervasive emphasis on faith throughout the Gospels (representative examples, table 5). As Wright expresses it, "for Jesus, 'faith' often seems to mean 'recognizing that God is decisively at work to bring the kingdom through Jesus.'"[3] Of course, this conviction necessitates a lifestyle evincing devotion to Jesus as Lord.

Further, the center of diatribe 1 features God's *grace*, which is extended to those who humble themselves and is sufficient to undo the carnage unleashed by the passions inherent to human nature. The further we traverse the Way of Jesus (and the more we read Jacob), the greater becomes our shame at the deep-seated self-centeredness that dominates our lives, and the more we can wonder at the divine grace that forgives and transforms us.

Table 5. Foci of Jacob's Chiasms: A Distillation of the Way of Jesus

Homily	"Hinge" teaching in Jacob	Teachings of Jesus
1	Poor, be glad, God exalts; rich, be glad, God humbles (1:9–11)	Blessed are the poor (Matt 5:3 // Luke 6:20); The greatest in the kingdom humbles himself (Matt 18:4; 23:12); Parable of the rich fool (Luke 12:13–21); Parable of Lazarus and the beggar (Luke 16:19–31); Hard for the rich to enter the kingdom (Mark 10:21–25 // Matt 19:21–24 // Luke 18:24–25)

---

3. As noted, footnotes 3 and 4 in chapter 6, and Wright, *John*, 167.

Summing Up

Table 5. Foci of Jacob's Chiasms: A Distillation of the Way of Jesus

Homily	"Hinge" teaching in Jacob	Teachings of Jesus
2	Looks, forgets; looks, does not forget (1:23b–25a)	"Listen if you have ears" (Matt 13:9, 13–14, 43); not hearing but doing (Matt 7:24–27 // Luke 6:49)
3	Poor, rich in faith; possess the kingdom (2:5)	Blessed are the poor (Matt 5:3 // Luke 6:20); Save riches in heaven (Matt 6:19–21 // Luke 12:32–34); Jesus has come with good news to the poor (Luke 4:18; Matt 11:5 // Luke 7:22)
4	Faith and actions work together; faith through actions, perfect (2:22)	Jesus healed those who had faith (e.g. Matt 9:22 // Mark 5:34 // Luke 8:48); "I have never found faith like this" (Matt 8:10); "You are a woman of great faith" (Matt 15:28); "What little faith, why did you doubt?" (Matt 14:31); "You don't have enough faith" (Matt 17:20); They did not have faith, he could do few mighty works (Matt 13:58 // Mark 6:6)
5a	The tongue like a ship's rudder; the tongue like a spark (3:5–6)	Whoever insults or calls his brother a fool will be judged (Matt 5:22); The mouth speaks what fills the heart (Matt 12:33–35 // Luke 6:43–45); Your words used to judge you (Matt 12:36–37); "These people honor me with their lips, but their hearts are far from me" (Matt 15:11, 17–20)

Table 5. Foci of Jacob's Chiasms: A Distillation of the Way of Jesus

Homily	"Hinge" teaching in Jacob	Teachings of Jesus
5b	Wisdom not from heaven; wisdom from earth, human nature, that is demonic (3:15)	Wise man, built on rock, foolish man on sand (Matt 7:24–27); God revealed to the unlearned what is hidden from the wise and learned (Matt 11:25); God's wisdom shown to be true (Matt 11:19 // Luke 5:37)
Diatribe 1	God's grace is stronger; God resists the proud, gives grace to the humble (4:6)	Happy are the humble (Matt 5:5); Those who humble themselves will be made great (Matt 18:4; 23:12 // Luke 18:14, 14:11)
Diatribe 2	If you judge the Law; you no longer obey the Law (4:11c–11e)	Obey the Law (Matt 5:17–19); Don't judge each other (Matt 7:1–5 // Luke 6:37–38, 41–42); Stop judging by appearances (John 7:24)
Diatribe 3	You should say, "If the Lord is willing we will do..." (4:15)	"Not everyone who says 'Lord' but those who do the will of my Father" (Matt 7:21); Whoever does the will of God (Matt 12:50 // Mark 3:35); Which of them did the will of his father? (Matt 21:31); "I have come to do the will of him who sent me" (John 6:38); "Your will be done" (Matt 6:10; 26:39 // Mark 14:36 // Luke 22:42)

SUMMING UP

Table 5. Foci of Jacob's Chiasms: A Distillation of the Way of Jesus

Homily	"Hinge" teaching in Jacob	Teachings of Jesus
Diatribe 4	You have not paid your workers; their cries have been heard by God (5:4)	"What you [teachers of the Law, Pharisees] have acquired by violence and selfishness" (Matt 23:25–26 // Luke 20:47); Parable of rich man and Lazarus (Luke 16:19–30); Parable of the compassionate employer[4] (Matt 20:1–16)
6	Above all, say "Yes or no" (5:12)	"Just say 'Yes' or 'No'" (Matt 5:33–37); Don't swear by temple or altar (Matt 23:16–22)

Jacob places emphasis on the destiny of those who are poor (homilies 1 and 3), humble (diatribe 1) and oppressed (diatribe 4). They are placed at the center of the chiasm each time they are mentioned. God's care for such people is assured. These references resonate amply with similar expressions in the Gospels.

Chiastic structures may have been developed as a means of demarcating homilies and as a mnemonic device to facilitate preaching, learning, and recalling. It has been noted that the Gospel of John appears to be composed extensively of chiasms.[5] It has been cogently argued that John was an eyewitness writer of the career of Jesus of Nazareth.[6] The Gospel of Mark also contains chiastic structures[7] and is likely to embody the teachings of another eyewitness (Peter).[8] Here, it is suggested that the letter of Jacob is composed of chiastic units that are the reflections of another man

---

4. Otherwise known as the parable of the workers in the vineyard, in which the owner gave a living wage to all workers, even to those could not do a day's work; see Bailey, *Jesus*, 355.

5. Breck, "Chiasmus in the Gospel," 72; Finlay, *Reading John's Gospel*.

6. Bauckham, *Eyewitnesses*, 410–11.

7. Stock, "Chiastic Awareness," 23, 26–27.

8. Bauckham, *Eyewitnesses*, 155–80.

who engaged directly with Jesus, and who was familiar with the Lord's teaching as it circulated in the earliest stratum of reported tradition.

These texts may have the common feature that they were transcriptions of original verbally transmitted sermons that proclaimed the Way of Jesus. The authors themselves had direct experience of the deeds and teaching of Jesus.

The great difference between John and Jacob is that John preached and wrote as an evangelist and pastor to promote enduring faith in Jesus.[9] Jacob preached and wrote as a pastor to encourage obedience and patience in those who were already resolute believers but suffering oppression for this same faith. In a world in which righteous living is devalued, if not despised, and the church adeptly compromises with the values of the world, Jacob's message remains as urgent as ever.

---

9. John 20:31.

Appendix 1

Jacob's Letter as One Extended Chiasm

A PLAUSIBLE ARRANGEMENT OF Jacob's letter, considered in its entirety, reveals a seven-fold chiastic pattern. This is depicted in figure 14, and details are outlined in table 6. A description of this chiastic structure follows below.

The first and last elements consider the difficulties that the believers face and appropriate responses to them. In the first element (1:2–18, A), the community faces the challenge of responding to trials. In the last element (5:1–18; A′), the believers face the challenge of suffering. In the first element, the trouble arises from the oppressing rich (*plousioi*) who are warned that they face only catastrophe. The last element is introduced by a brief chiasm (5:1–6) in which Jacob takes the rich (*plousioi*) to task for their oppression of the helpless, and again warns them of God's inevitable judgment. This parallelism makes it clear that the earlier chiasm (5:1–6) is intended to accompany the concluding one (5:7–18) and functions as a preamble to the latter. The response to this painful experience is resolute endurance, patience, and prayer, as stated in both A and A′ elements.

Appendix 1

A 1:2-18 being faithful under trials
   B 1:19-27 hearing and doing – resisting the world
     C 2:1-13 warning against prejudice
       D 2:14-26 faith and actions
     C' 3:1-18 warning against misuse of the tongue
   B' 4:1-17 speaking and doing – friendship with the world
A' 5:1-18 being patient and prayerful under trials

Figure 14. Jacob's Letter Is Structured as a Single Extensive Chiasm

The second and second to last elements of the letter are concerned with listening and doing (1:19-27, B) and speaking and doing (4:1-17, B').[1] The necessary response to God's word requires attentive listening to it, issuing in obedience (the *doing* of it; B). Our talk is often wrong-headed, indicative of selfish priorities, and to order our lives rightly requires that we reorientate the *doings* of our lives (B'). In each element, Jacob warns his readers to avoid the insidious effects and entanglements of *the world*—here used in the sense of society opposed to God (1:27 in B, and 4:4 in B', twice).

The third pair of elements is concerned with possible abuses of other people that can arise—yes, even in the church. We are warned against prejudicial treatment of others (especially in the context of the worshiping community; 2:1-13, C) and against dismissive or destructive use of the tongue, that is, hurtful pronouncements about others (especially in the context of the learning community; 3:1-18, C'). Both parallels indicate these behaviors are evils that will bring the perpetrators under God's judgment. Jacob reminds his readers that prejudice, whether in acted or verbal forms, amounts to dismissive treatment of our fellow believers. Such abuse of others is all the more heinous because those whom we might despise or deprecate possess the supreme dignity of being inheritors of God's promised kingdom (2:5 in C) and of being made in God's own image (3:9 in C'). That person we might be tempted to despise, and even reject, is a child of the King!

---

1. English translations seem to vary in the way they express the underlying idea of *doing* (related to Greek *poiesis*), of which there is a concentration of four instances in each element.

Table 6. Parallel Features in the Chiastic Structure of Jacob's Letter

Element	Section	Specific parallels	References
A	1:2–18	trials	1:2, 3, 12, 13
		the oppressing rich—will fade away	1:11
		endurance	1:3, 4, 12
		asking God	1:5, 6
B	1:19–27	need for doing, *poiesis*	1:22, 23, 25 (twice)
		avoid corruption of the world	1:27
C	2:1–13	prejudicial treatment of others	2:1–4, 6, 9
		an evil	2:4
		liable to judgment	2:12, 13
		dignity of others, possess the kingdom	2:5
D	2:14–26	faith and action	2:14, 17, 18 (three times), 20, 22 (twice), 24, 26
C'	3:1–18	dismissive speech about others	3:6, 9
		an evil	3:6, 8
		liable to judgment	3:1
		dignity of others, image of God	3:9
B'	4:1–17	need for doing, *poiesis*	4:11, 13, 15, 17
		avoid friendship with the world	4:4 (twice)
A'	5:1–18	suffering	5:10
		the oppressing rich—will be destroyed	5:1–6 (previous chiasm)
		patience; endurance	5:7 (twice), 8, 10; 10
		prayer	5:14–18

The central element of the letter (2:14–26, D; unpaired) describes the relationship between God and the members of the community. It is the homily on faith evinced by action. The paired terms faith and action are given together ten times, a concentration of key words that reinforces the impact of this section as the hub of the letter. Authentic faith that makes people righteous before

APPENDIX 1

God (vv. 21, 23, 24, 25) must be demonstrated by actions. The rest of the letter is but commentary of this fundamental fact, which is stressed by every contributor to the New Testament.

As an interesting aside, it seems that the chiastic organization of Jacob's letter fits closely with the chapter boundaries. This correspondence is especially interesting in the more complex second half of the document. The chapter divisions were thus inserted very judiciously.[2]

---

2. Given the structure proposed for Jacob's letter (fig. 14, table 6), the hypothesis presented itself that ch. 4 might in fact be a single chiasm to balance 1:19–27. Indeed, late analysis identified a strongly chiastic pattern in ch. 4. This reinforces the outline of Jacob's letter as depicted above. The three small sections of ch. 4 may be read, not merely as independent "mini-chiasms," but as a unit paralleled with section 1:19–27.

A(a) ¹⁻²ᵃ harmful speech: fights, quarrels
  (b) ²ᵇ what you do not have
  (c) ²ᶜ asking God—our wants
  (d) ³ underlying sin: selfish motives
      B ⁴ᵃ don't you know—world's friend is God's enemy?
         C(a) ⁴ᵇ⁻⁵ whoever is the world's friend becomes God's enemy
           (b) ⁶ God gives grace
              D ⁷ᵃ injunction: submit to God
                 E ⁷ᵇ⁻⁸ᵃ resist Devil, he will flee; come to God, he will come
                    F ⁸ᵇ wash, purify from sin
                    F' ⁹ lament over sin
                 E' ¹⁰ be humble before God, he will exalt
              D' ¹¹ᵃ injunction: don't criticize
         C'(a') ¹¹ᵇ whoever criticizes/judges another criticizes/judges the law
           (b') ¹²ᵃ God alone is judge
      B' ¹²ᵇ who do you think you are—judge?
A'(a') ¹³ harmful speech: boasting
  (b') ¹⁴ what you do not know
  (c') ¹⁵ asking God—God's will
  (d') ¹⁶⁻¹⁷ underlying sin: pride

APPENDIX 2

CHIASMS WITHIN A CHIASM

THE FINAL LARGE CHIASM (5:7–18) may have been assembled from two smaller units. Each of these units seems to have had the property of a chiasm.

The first of these has to do with the importance of patience (fig. 15). The first and last elements acknowledge the need for patience and provide the foundation—the Lord himself—for exercising this virtue. Patience is needed until the Lord comes (v. 7a, A) and is justified by the Lord's mercy and compassion (v. 11c, A′). The second and penultimate elements provide classical examples of people renowned for their patience. Jacob describes the horticulturalist, whose labors are rewarded (hopefully) by seasonal rain (v. 7b, B), and the paradigmatic sufferer Job, who lived to see the Lord address his agonized cries (v. 11b, B′). The next elements personalize the imperative to be patient, urging the readers to expect great outcomes (v. 8a, C), and citing the prophets upon whom their discipleship is modeled, who are now revered and recognized as blessed (vv. 10–11a, C′). Suffering is not interminable. The time of relief is close, the climactic day when the Lord (v. 8b, D) and Judge (v. 9b, D′) will appear. The practical implication of all this is at the center of the chiasm. The readers must not allow the current difficulties to create friction between them (v. 9a, E), for that would incur God's judgment (v. 9a, E′).

APPENDIX 2

A ⁷ᵃ be patient, brothers, until the Lord comes
  B ⁷ᵇ see farmer's patience—waits for land to produce crops; waits patiently for autumn, spring rains
    C ⁸ᵃ you also be patient; keep your hopes high
      D ⁸ᵇ the day of the Lord's coming is near
        E ⁹ᵃ don't complain against one another
        E' so that God will not judge you
      D' ⁹ᵇ the Judge is near, ready to appear
    C' ¹⁰⁻¹¹ᵃ the prophets spoke in the Lord's name; patient endurance under suffering; happy because endured
  B' ¹¹ᵇ you have heard of Job's patience—the Lord provided for him in the end
A' ¹¹ᶜ the Lord is full of mercy and compassion

Figure 15. Patience Under Pressure

And finally, the homily on prayer (fig. 16). The chiasm is bracketed by the need to pray (v. 13, A) and the effectiveness of prayer in the case of Elijah (v. 18, A'). This pertains to those who are sick in the church (v. 14, B), and to Elijah in his confrontation with corrupt rulers (v. 17, B'). Such prayer unleashes God's healing (v. 15a, C) and, in general, God's power (v. 16d, C') in the life of the believer. Healing is reiterated (vv. 15b, D; 16c, D') with the promise (in the former element) that forgiveness will be granted. The central elements (as in the previous chiasm, fig. 15) specify what the believers must do for *one another* to receive spiritual and physical health: confess sin (v. 16a, E) and pray (v. 16b, E').

A ¹³ in trouble? pray; happy? sing praises
  B ¹⁴ sick? send for the elders, who will pray, anoint with oil in the Lord's name
    C ¹⁵ᵃ prayer in faith will heal the sick
      D ¹⁵ᵇ the Lord will restore their health, forgive their sins
        E ¹⁶ᵃ confess sins to one another
        E' ¹⁶ᵇ pray for one another
      D' ¹⁶ᶜ so that you will be healed
    C' ¹⁶ᵈ prayer of a good person: powerful, effective
  B' ¹⁷ Elijah was like us; prayed earnestly that there would be no rain, no rain fell for three and a half years
A' ¹⁸ again he prayed, sky gave rain, earth gave crops

Figure 16. Praying When Troubled

Chiasms Within a Chiasm

It is possible that Jacob had a sermon on patience and one on prayer. He was concerned that the trials to which his flock were exposed could lead to outbreaks of irritability and so disrupt its unity. The two sermons were amalgamated into one. The aim was to make sure that divisions, and the concomitant emotional and physical ailments that often ensue from then, did not arise. When under protracted pressure, members of the community must resist the tendency to complain (fig. 15). When reduced to illness, they must confess their sins and pray for each other (fig. 16). Such responses are healing, both in the body of the individual and in the body of Christ, and they work effectively to suppress those fissiparous tendencies.

BIBLIOGRAPHY

Alexander, Denis, and Alister McGrath, eds. *Coming to Faith Through Dawkins*. Grand Rapids: Kregel, 2023.

Ash, Sydney, et al. "The Neural Correlates of Narcissism: Is There a Connection with Desire for Fame and Celebrity Worship?" *Brain Sciences* 13 (2023) 1499. https://doi.org/10.3390/brainsci13101499.

Bailey, Kenneth E. *Jesus Through Middle Eastern Eyes*. Downers Grove, IL: InterVarsity, 2008.

Barclay, William. *Letters of James and Peter*. Edinburgh: Saint Andrew Press, 1960.

Bauckham, Richard. *Jesus and the Eyewitnesses*. Grand Rapids: Eerdmans, 2006.

Blaiklock, Edward M. *Psalms for Living: Psalms 1–72*. Commentary on the Psalms 1. London: Scripture Union, 1977.

Breck, John. "Biblical Chiasmus: Exploring Structure for Meaning." *Biblical Theology Bulletin: Journal of Bible and Culture* 17 (1987) 70–74.

———. "Chiasmus in the Gospel of John." *Sacra Scripta* 1 (2004) 72–90.

Bruce, F. F. *Israel and the Nations*. Revised ed. Exeter, UK: Paternoster, 1983.

Cambridge Dictionary. "Homily." https://dictionary.cambridge.org/dictionary/english/homily.

de Gruchy, John W. *Christianity and Democracy*. Cambridge: Cambridge University Press, 1995.

Drane, John W. *The Life of the Early Church*. Tring, UK: Lion, 1982.

Evans, Craig A. *Ancient Texts for New Testament Studies*. Grand Rapids: Baker Academic, 2011.

———. *From Jesus to the Church*. Louisville: Westminster John Knox, 2014.

Finlay, Graeme J. *A Way of Reading John's Gospel*. Eugene, OR: Wipf & Stock, 2024.

Harrison, Peter. *The Territories of Science and Religion*. Chicago: University of Chicago Press, 2015.

Hart, David Bentley. *Atheist Delusions: The Christian Revolution and Its Fashionable Enemies*. New Haven, CT: Yale University Press, 2009.

Hauerwas, Stanley, and William H. Willimon. *Resident Aliens*. Nashville: Abingdon, 1989.

BIBLIOGRAPHY

Kaiser, Walter C., Jr., et al. *Hard Sayings of the Bible*. Downers Grove, IL: InterVarsity, 1996.

König, Adrio. *The Eclipse of Christ in Eschatology: Toward a Christ-Centered Approach*. Blackwood, AU: New Creation, 2007.

Louth, Andrew, ed. *Early Christian Writings: The Apostolic Fathers*. Translated by Maxwell Staniforth. Harmondsworth, UK: Penguin, 1968.

McCoy, Brad. "Chiasmus: An Important Structural Device Commonly Found in Biblical Literature." *Chafer Theological Seminary Journal* 9 (Fall 2003) 18–34.

Stock, Augustine. "Chiastic Awareness and Education in Antiquity." *Biblical Theology Bulletin: Journal of Bible and Culture* 14 (1984) 23–27.

Vine, W. E. *An Expository Dictionary of New Testament Words*. London: Oliphants, 1940.

Walker, H. H., and N. W. Lund. "The Literary Structure of the Book of Habakkuk." *Journal of Biblical Literature* 53 (1934) 355–70.

Wenham, Gordon J. "The Coherence of the Flood Narrative." *Vetus Testamentum* 28.3 (1978) 336–48.

———. *Exploring the Old Testament: The Pentateuch*. London: SPCK, 2003.

Whiston, William W., trans. *The New Complete Works of Josephus*. Commentary by Paul L. Maier. Grand Rapids: Kregel, 1999.

White, R. E. O. *Biblical Ethics*. In *Christian Ethics*, 1–256. Leominster, UK: Gracewing, 1994.

———. *Insights of History*. In *Christian Ethics*, 1–442. Leominster, UK: Gracewing, 1994.

Wilson, Mark. "James or Jacob in the Bible: Giving Jacob His Due." Biblical Archaeology Society, April 24, 2025. https://www.biblicalarchaeology.org/daily/biblical-topics/bible-versions-and-translations/james-or-jacob-in-the-bible/.

Wright, N. T. *Jesus and the Victory of God*. London: SPCK, 1996.

———. *John for Everyone: Part 1*. The New Testament for Everyone. London: SPCK, 2002.

Wright, N. T., and Michael F. Bird. *The New Testament in Its World*. London: SPCK, 2019.

Zsila, Agnes, et al. "Prevalence of Celebrity Worship: Development and Application of the Short Version of the Celebrity Attitude Scale (CAS-7) on a Large-Scale Representative Sample." *Journal of Behavioral Addictions* 13 (2024) 463–72. doi:10.1556/2006.2024.00019.

INDEX

Abraham, 16, 37, 38
actions, 3, 21, 28 notes 7 and 8, 34, 35, 37, 44, 63, 74
Acts of the Apostles, 5, 18
agape, 31
Albinus, 47n1
animals, 41; animal nature, 45
Annas I, 47n1, 57n18
Annas II, 47n1, 56, 57n18
anointing (with oil), 3
aparche, 23n7
Aramaic, 10
ascension, 8

Barclay, William, 25, 44
Bird, Michael, 10, 62
blessed, 11, 22n3, 29, 43, 65, 75
Breck, John, 18
brothers, 6, 18–20, 26, 30, 46, 59

celebrity, 33
chairein, 5
chiasm, chiasmus, x, 13, 15–20, 22, 26, 28, 36, 37, 41, 42, 46, 47, 49, 50–52, 59, 60, 62, 65, 66, 69, 71, 75, 76
church, 1, 3–5, 10, 11, 32, 39, 51, 63, 76
confess, confession, 60n1, 61, 62, 76, 77
Council, see *Sanhedrin*

covenant, 9, 16, 26n1, 38, 40, 63
creation, 15, 23, 40, 63; new creation, 22
criticizing, criticism, 20, 51, 52

David, 12n1, 14, 15
Davids, Peter, 4, 24, 43n8
deceive, deception, 23, 24, 28, 29
diaspora, 2
diatribe, 10, 32, 65, 66, 69
Didache, 64
dipsuchos, 64
doing, 28, 29, 54, 63, 72
doubt, 24, 25, 29
Drane, John, 2, 3

ekklesia, 9, 11
Elijah, 76
endure, endurance, 37, 65, 71
epistemon, 43
Evans, Craig, 6, 10, 11

faith, 3, 8, 9, 21, 25, 28, 32, 34–39, 44, 61, 63–66, 73
Festus, 47n1
fire, 41, 42
freedom, 25, 28, 49, 55
fruit, 42n7, 43, 44, 60, 62n5

Galilee, 3, 10
gifts, 23n7, 24, 25, 31n21

God, 9, 11, 12, 14–16, 19, 22, 24, 25, 27, 28, 31–33, 34n1, 35–40, 43, 45, 47–56, 58, 62n4, 63–66, 73
grace, 37, 49–51, 66
Greek (language), 1, 6, 9, 10, 27, 28n8, 72n1

Habakkuk, 13
Hart, David, 55
Hebrew, 1, 12, 17; language, 62; Scriptures, 2, 6, 13, 15, 26n1; writings, 7
Hegesippus, 8
High Priest, 47, 57n18
hinge, 15, 18, 21, 54, 55, 59, 65, 66
homily, 18n20, 19, 22, 26, 32, 34, 35, 39, 40, 42, 43, 45–48, 51, 53–56, 58, 59, 60n2, 65, 73, 76
horse, 41
humble, 50, 51, 53, 64–66, 69

Iakob(os), 1
image of God, 40, 72
inverted parallelisms, see *chiasm*
Isaac, 37, 38
Israel, 3, 11, 35, 36, 58n20, 66

Jacob (as patriarch), 1, 2; as writer of the letter, 1–11, 18, 20, 22, 46, 47, 56, 57n18, 65, 70, 77
James, see *Jacob (as writer)*
jealousy, 44
Jerusalem, 57, 10; church in, 1, 3, 6, 10, 11
Jesus, 1–4, 7–11, 20, 22–26, 27n2, 30–32, 34–36, 42, 43, 45, 47, 53, 56, 65, 66, 69, 70
Jews, 2, 3, 11; Hellenistic, 10
Job, 61, 75
Jonathan, son of Annas, 57n18
Josephus, 47n1

judge, judging, 46, 52; God as Judge, 9, 15, 52, 75

karpos, see *fruit*
Kingdom of God, 11, 25n10, 30, 32, 33, 35, 53, 65, 66, 72; law of, 30

last days, 9
law, 31, 52, 53, 64, 65; Jewish, 3, 6, 58n20; of love, 28–30
lawbreaker, 31, 52
likeness (image) of God, 40, 72
listening, 6, 26, 28, 29, 72
love, 27–31, 34, 36, 37, 49n6, 52, 64
Luther, Martin, 34n1

Matthew, gospel of, 3, 4, 30n1
Noah, 15, 16

Old Testament, 1, 2, 15
palistrophe, 15
parallel(ism), 12, 13, 17–19, 23, 24, 26, 37, 41, 44, 52, 54
parousia, 9
patience, 26, 59–62, 71, 75, 77
Paul, 3, 23n3, 31n2, 35, 42n6, 45n15
persecution, 8, 11, 22, 25
Peter, 10, 23, 56, 69
plousios, 20, 32n4, 71
plutocracy, 20, 24, 31, 57n18
poiesis, 72n1
(the) poor, 11, 20, 24, 25, 32, 57, 65
pray, prayer, 59–62, 71, 76, 77
prejudice, 30, 32, 44, 72
presbuteroi, 9
pride, 52, 54, 55
Psalms, 13
pseudonymity, 9

quarrelling, 20, 50, 51

Rahab, 36, 37
rains, 60, 75

Index

receive, 23, 24, 29, 50, 76
religion, 27
repentance, 48, 51, 64
resurrection, 8, 11, 23n7
(the) rich, 3, 20, 24, 25, 31, 32, 46, 56, 57, 64, 65, 71
righteous, righteousness, 9, 14, 15, 37, 43, 45, 49, 58n20, 73

Sanhedrin, 20, 47, 56
Septuagint, 6
Sermon on the Mount, 4
shalom, 62
Shema, 36
ship, 41
sophos, 43
spirit, 44, 49, 50, 53; the Holy Spirit, 9, 23n7, 44, 49, 50
Spurgeon, Charles, 32
synagoge, 11
synagogue, 3

teacher(s), 19, 39, 42–44
Theophilus, son of Annas, 57n18
threskeia, 27
tongue, 20, 39, 41–43, 46, 51–53, 60, 72
Torah, 2, 26n1
trials, 22, 65, 71, 77
truth, 23, 44, 59, 60, 62

unity, 8, 59, 77

Wenham, Gordon, 15
White, R. E. O., 4, 30n1
widows and orphans, 26
will (of God), 48, 54, 56, 62, 64
Wilson, Mark, 1
wisdom, x, 19, 23, 24, 39, 42–46, 64, 65; wisdom books, 2, 6
world, 8, 11, 19, 20, 27, 39, 43, 45, 46, 48, 64, 65, 70, 72
Wright, Tom, 10, 62, 66
Wyclif, John, 1

www.ingramcontent.com/pod-product-compliance
Lightning Source LLC
Chambersburg PA
CBHW060423090426
42734CB00011B/2419